TEACHING AND LEADING WITH

EMOTIONAL INTELLIGENCE

TEACHING AND LEADING WITH

EMOTIONAL

INTELLIGENCE

A DILEMMA-BASED CASEBOOK
for EARLY CARE and EDUCATION

PEGGY DALY PIZZO

with Teresa Gonczy O'Rourke and Ed Greene

FOREWORD BY EDWARD F. ZIGLER

TEACHERS COLLEGE PRESS

TEACHERS COLLEGE | COLUMBIA UNIVERSITY

NEW YORK AND LONDON

Published by Teachers College Press, 1234 Amsterdam Avenue, New York, NY 10027

Copyright © 2018 by Teachers College, Columbia University

Cover photo: Caiaimage / Robert Daly, Getty Images

Library of Congress Cataloging-in-Publication Data is available at loc.gov

ISBN 978-0-8077-5884-7 (paper)
ISBN 978-0-8077-7675-9 (ebook)

Printed on acid-free paper
Manufactured in the United States of America

25 24 23 22 21 20 19 18   8 7 6 5 4 3 2 1

Contents

PART II. CASES ON EARLY CHILDHOOD LEADERSHIP

Foreword

You have begun a book that has the potential to profoundly change the way we educate teachers and leaders in the field of early care and education and how we should organize professional development around key concepts—like the understanding that the whole child matters.

Teaching and Leading with Emotional Intelligence: A Dilemma-Based Casebook for Early Care and Education restores balance to the way we initially prepare teachers and leaders and continually engage them in high-quality professional development. The accountability movement shapes what is taught in early care and education programs by emphasizing quantifiable, academically oriented skills, so that children can be tested and resulting test scores can be used to demonstrate program "results." Results do matter, as they indicate a good investment by parents and taxpayers. But decades of research on high-quality early childhood education demonstrates that socioemotional skills are lasting results that translate into meaningful schooling and life outcomes—greater rates of high school completion and participation in postsecondary education, for example.

This excellent book will restore balance to our school readiness accountability initiatives. It demonstrates the growth of the whole child, using well-written, research-based portrayals of teachers and leaders displaying emotional intelligence and fostering its growth in children, teachers, and leaders. This book also restores balance to the way we educate teachers and leaders. Too much teacher training is didactic, with lectures delivered in the hopes that large amounts of information will be absorbed and result in better, more effective teachers. Peggy Daly Pizzo is helping to pioneer an approach more likely to result in skill development—dilemma-based teaching cases that engage the mind and heart of students in authentic learning and skill development.

There is a deeper current flowing through this book: the fundamental belief that nothing matters more to a healthy, just, and prosperous society than investing in and providing access to high-quality early care and family support for all children and families. Decades of research are clear: The experiences of the first 8 years of life profoundly shape the rest of a human being's life.

I have dedicated my entire adult life to the goal of paving the way for all children—not just the affluent few—to experience the best possible start in life. In the early 1960s, I helped establish the Head Start and the Early Head Start programs. Also, I inaugurated the Federal Office of Child Development, now the Administration for Children, Youth, and Families (ACYF), which is part of the U.S. Department of Health and Human Services that runs the Head Start program and administers grants to states for child care services for low-income families. Later, I founded the Bush Center for Child Development and Social Policy at Yale University, now the Edward Zigler Center for Child Development and Social Policy, which has given birth to innumerable empirical research studies intended to infuse policy decisions with sound knowledge about child development.

Peggy Daly Pizzo is a long-esteemed colleague who has dedicated her life to these same goals. I first met Peggy when she worked in the Domestic Policy Staff of President Carter's White House and when I was asked by the President to chair the 15th Anniversary Head Start Committee. Peggy's competence and integrity impressed me and I asked her to serve as an adjunct faculty member at the Bush Center.

Our paths also crossed at innumerable junctions, including when she served as a senior program associate and I served on the board at what is now Zero to Three. She authored chapters for textbooks on child development and social policy that I coedited and we worked together on important initiatives, including the passage of the Family and Medical Leave Act. We continued to work together when Peggy was at Harvard University and also when she moved to Stanford University.

This excellent book is the fruition of many scholarly exchanges we've had over the years; it reflects our joint commitment to the best possible lives for all America's young children. Indeed, I helped her get this book started. While engaged in seminal thinking about what young children most need to thrive and learn even when confronting enormous adversity, Peggy visited me at Yale. She was debating writing a book about resilience and emotional intelligence, rightly understanding that both these abilities are fundamental to a child's success in preschool, school, and life.

I strongly recommended that Peggy adopt emotional intelligence as the organizing concept for this casebook. She did. The result: an intelligent, thoughtful book that illustrates how early childhood teachers, center directors, and agency leaders can use emotional intelligence to foster the growth of this essential life skill in young children and in the adults who have the power to shape their lives for good or for ill.

These in-depth teaching cases should be read and widely used throughout every institution of higher education where faculty prepare practitioners to work at every level of early care and education program and policy. Every faculty member and community-based trainer can use these cases to deepen their students' knowledge about child development and best practice in early care and education, as well as to promote the skills of critical reasoning, analysis, and group discussion.

Even better is that students will be fully engaged by these lively, well-written narratives and drawn into both deeper levels of thought and broader arcs of awareness through research-intensive narratives that examine such critical cases as perspective-taking and sharing; linguistic and cultural differences in temperamentally reserved children; challenging behaviors and the resultant risk of preschool expulsion faced by highly energetic, intense children; and inadequacy of workforce compensation that result in challenges to leaders trying to run high-quality programs.

But Peggy doesn't just describe or illustrate problems—she highlights solutions. This book is a valuable asset in every program of practitioner preparation and ongoing professional development—all students and instructors will love its original and positive approach and admire its immersion in both scholarship and practical lives and issues. It will translate into many benefits for actual children and families—the goals for which Peggy and I have worked all our adult lives. I cannot recommend too highly this superb, well-written book.

—*Edward F. Zigler*

Preface

I came to the writing of this book because of the Dalai Lama. I had been experiencing a prolonged period of poor health, and I was searching for inspiring and resilient public figures and books that would help me cope best with these health challenges.

But I was also spending a great deal of time reflecting on key questions related to the effectiveness of early childhood education. I kept asking myself, "When a child has a successful experience in an early childhood program, what matters most in ensuring that success? What is foundational? What has to happen in order for the child to be able to learn, to make friends, to use her skills and abilities well?"

I began reading some of the books by the Dalai Lama and came across the concept of "training the mind." With neuroscientists and leading Buddhist scholars, the Dalai Lama had established the Mind and Life Institute, and I began to read some of the materials on their website (www.mindandlife.org). I stumbled across Daniel Goleman and his book *Emotional Intelligence* (1995). As I read it, I thought: "This is it! This is the foundational ability that must develop well in order for a child to acquire skills in early math, early literacy, and other areas."

I reflected that a child needed to be able to control impulses, to problem-solve, to manage attention, and to regulate emotions and behavior. Abilities like this would enable the child to take advantage of the key ingredients in effective early childhood education: a well-ordered, excellent classroom environment and skilled teachers. I was aware that developmentally appropriate practice (DAP), the widely used research-based framework developed by the National Association for the Education of Young Children (NAEYC) to guide early childhood teaching practice, emphasizes the importance of fostering these kinds of abilities. I felt supported, then, by the thought leaders of the respected national membership organization to which I had belonged since the 1970s. As I was reflecting, however, public policy and parental pressures were converging to exalt the importance of academic skills in young children to the exclusion of social and emotional abilities. The No Child Left Behind Act (now the Every Student Succeeds Act) was requiring the testing of students in grades 3 and above for academic skills. This powerful law tied federal funding to test performance, exerting pressures for an educational laser-like focus on purely academic skills. I wanted to lend my voice to pushing back against those pressures.

So I decided to propose to my mentor, Ed Zigler of Yale University, one of the founders of the Head Start program, that I do some writing in this area. He was supportive and introduced me to Roger Weissberg, one of the founders of the Collaborative for Academic, Social, and Emotional Learning (CASEL). I found the CASEL framework for social and emotional learning (SEL) to be a well-thought-out depiction of five key elements needed for emotional and social intelligence: (1) self-awareness, (2) social awareness, (3) self-management or self-regulation, (4) relationship management, and (5) responsible decision making. Ed also introduced me to Marilou Hyson who was then working at NAEYC. Marilou had just completed revising her book *The Emotional Development of Young Children* (2004), which I read with great pleasure and appreciation for its insights.

Roger Weissberg introduced me to Susanne Denham, a leading scholar in the area of emotional development of young children. Her superb research has greatly informed the development of the teaching cases in this book. As Susanne and I discussed the CASEL framework, which had been developed for children above the age of 5, we modified the fifth element, responsible decision making, to illustrate behaviors that were more appropriate to 3- and 4-year olds. We decided that the wording about responsible decision making should be "problem solving leading toward responsible decision making." We both felt it was inappropriate to expect 3-year-olds to shoulder more than the simplest responsibilities.

I also asked the late Gwen Morgan of Wheelock College, a longtime thought leader in early childhood matters, to connect me with any individuals working in the field of emotional intelligence. She connected me with Holly Elisa Bruno, who had just published *What You Need to Lead an Early Childhood Program: Emotional Intelligence in Practice* (2012).

I also turned to T. Berry Brazelton of Harvard University, a longtime mentor and friend, whose books beautifully portrayed children successfully struggling with difficult temperaments to develop emotional and social skills. He introduced me to Joshua Sparrow, MD, with whom he was directing the Brazelton Touchpoints Center at Harvard.

In addition to consulting with these individuals and reading their works, I began to read in depth the research literature in the field of emotional and social intelligence. Ultimately, I read several hundred studies, policy requirements, and program guidance documents, many of which are listed in the Recommended Reading and References at the end of this book.

I approached a colleague, Yolanda Garcia, who was then responsible for overseeing training and professional development for more than eight thousand providers in Santa Clara County, where Stanford University is located. I proposed to her that I continue to review some of the literature on emotional and social intelligence, as background for the development of training materials. She was quite supportive, saying that she recognized that social and emotional learning was absolutely critical in early care and education classrooms. At the time, she was managing a large contract with First 5 Santa Clara County, an agency which provides funds throughout the county for services for children ages 0–5. Yolanda in turn introduced me to Jolene Smith, the executive director of First 5 at the time. They launched this project by providing me with some initial funding.

After a long period of time reading books, articles, and other documents, I recognized that I longed to get out into actual classrooms. So I went to Bing Nursery School, Stanford's NAEYC-accredited laboratory preschool. There I saw the most intensely beautiful exchanges between teachers and children. With the support of Jennifer Winters, the executive director of Bing; Beth Wise, the school's associate director; and Chia-wa Yeh, their research coordinator, I began doing 90-minute observations in Bing classrooms each week, using an ethnographic approach. I dictated parts of each in-depth observation that captured how highly skilled the teachers were. As I observed in Bing classrooms, I saw that the teachers interacted with the children precisely in ways that research indicated would lead to the foundations of healthy social and emotional development. I could also see the teachers using highly skilled interactions to remedy problem areas in a child's development.

Bing is a very high quality laboratory preschool serving primarily middle- and upper-middle-income children. It is an ideal setting to document best practice and shines forth as an ideal that could be realized in any setting for young children, if the appropriate resources of funding, knowledge, and skills were made available throughout our society to early childhood programs. I was (and am) deeply grateful to Bing's teachers and leaders for showing me what ideal practice in a well-resourced preschool looks like. But I knew I also needed to carry out classroom observations in settings where staff struggled to achieve best practice despite the lack of resources. So, for a long period of time, I observed highly skilled teachers in a mixed-income, nonprofit, NAEYC-accredited program: St. Elizabeth's Day Home, in San Jose. St. Elizabeth's served many immigrant children with highly dedicated staff, but limited financial resources. Unfortunately, several years after I began observing there, due to the shortage of public funding for a program like theirs, St. Elizabeth's had to close their doors and shut down.

In addition to research review and classroom observation at Bing and at St. Elizabeth's, I interviewed the teachers and directors of both programs. From these interviews I came to understand the philosophy, values, and culture of each center and the personal philosophies of each professional. Deeply infused with the philosophy of NAEYC's developmentally appropriate practice (DAP), and of NAEYC's code of ethics, the teachers and leaders in both programs exemplified the best thinking in the early childhood field.

As I thought about the best ways to approach the professional development of teachers, I came across work by Judy Shulman, who had developed teaching cases for more than 15 years at WestEd, a national nonprofit organization that promotes excellence in education through research and training. I became thoroughly intrigued by the potential of using a case-based approach to professional development, instead of relying principally on a didactic approach. I reached out to Judy, and she became a valuable mentor. I decided to develop six in-depth teaching cases that would fundamentally portray highly skilled teachers taking quite challenging moments and scenarios in classrooms and transforming them into opportunities for growth of social–emotional skills.

I knew that the teaching cases should present issues and dilemmas that teachers commonly experienced in classrooms. Therefore, I decided to develop the first two cases with a focus on (1) the development of skills related to problem solving and sharing and (2) the challenges experienced by a monolingual child in a classroom where his language is not spoken by the teachers or director of the program. Out of this decision arose "Tomas, Arthur, and Sharing: Resolving Conflicts" (Case 1) and "Ming: A Mystery Story for Teachers and Student Teachers" (Case 2). These cases, along with the four others I discuss, are summarized in the introduction to this book.

After researching and writing these two cases, I went to the Institute for Human and Social Development (IHSD) in San Mateo County, a county near Stanford University. IHSD is the Head Start grantee for this county, serving over 800 low-income children in 27 sites throughout the county. I went there to propose doing classroom observations of teacher–child interaction in Head Start centers in order to help develop the remaining teaching cases. However, IHSD's then professional development manager, Sandy Baba, and the executive director, Angel Barrios, talked me into doing a case that would focus on the leaders of this large agency. Called "content managers," these leaders possess special expertise in the comprehensive areas of child and family need that Head Start requires programs to address: health, mental health, nutrition, family engagement, early childhood education, and support for special needs children and their families.

Out of an extensive review of research and policy related to Head Start, and an intensive period of interviewing and listening to these content managers, as well as participation in their leadership meetings, came the next two teaching cases I wrote. Focused on the extraordinary challenges facing Head Start leadership, these cases—"Coming To Ground" (Case 5) and "Crises and Compassion" (Case 6)—are intended to illustrate adult social and emotional intelligence in leaders of large agencies dealing with a continuous stream of crises. In our profoundly underfunded early childhood system, leaders of large early care and education agencies confront multiple crises on a daily basis.

In writing these cases I was also drawn back into the world of policy issues, a world that I had inhabited for over 20 years in Washington, DC. What drew me back was the recognition that teacher compensation in Head Start (and in other early childhood programs) was still woefully inadequate, despite several decades of research-based advocacy to increase compensation and improve teacher preparation and ongoing professional development. From my field research I could see that inadequate teacher compensation is a root cause of poor quality—and a huge impediment to efforts to upgrade that quality by even the most dedicated and skilled staff. As a result, I decided to focus these two cases on the highly relevant policy issue of low wages as a basic cause of crises, as well as the use of social and emotional intelligence by leaders.

Having completed those two cases, I turned my attention back to teacher–child interaction. The development of executive function—the ability to plan, organize, keep things in working memory, and juggle tasks and information—is an essential foundation in all learning. So in the next teaching case I delved into the development of self-regulation and executive function. I had observed teachers doing a superb job of fostering these abilities even when they were working with highly active, highly intense, impulsive children who were very challenging to interact with. I decided to merge an in-depth look at the development of executive function and self-regulation with the highly relevant policy issues surrounding the expulsion from preschool of young children with challenging behaviors, especially boys of color. From this decision arose the case, "Sky-High Energy in Classroom Five" (Case 3). To write this case, I decided to seek coauthors and reached out to Teresa Gonczy O'Rourke, an independent consultant and recent alumnae of the Harvard Graduate School of Education, where she had studied with Jack Shankoff, founding director of the development of science-based materials on executive function. I also asked Ed Greene, a longtime friend and colleague, to coauthor this case with me. Ed has served as a leader with NAEYC, the National Black Child Development Institute, and other national organizations and has invaluable insights into understanding and responding to challenging behaviors in young children generally. He also deeply understands the issues surrounding challenging behaviors in boys of color.

When this case was completed I turned my attention to the issues surrounding child abuse. In my field research I had observed teachers reclaiming a child stuck in traumatized behavior. So after reviewing the research related to childhood trauma, I developed the case "Roberto and Maria: Two Children Dealing with Trauma" (Case 4). In writing this case, I tried to show what I actually observed: emotionally intelligent adults working with children and their families in exceptionally challenging circumstances.

This, then, is how these cases evolved. Two streams of conviction infused the decisions that I made about writing them. I am convinced that social–emotional skills can and should be taught in early care and education programs. I am also convinced that a case-based approach to the development of teacher and leader skills is an exceptionally valuable professional development approach to fostering these skills in children. I believe that the case-based approach is an important complement to the more didactic presentations that characterize typical approaches to higher education.

Acknowledgments

I'd like to express gratitude to the many individuals and entities who helped me write this book. Stanford University, First 5 Santa Clara County, Jill and John Freidenrich, Maddy and Isaac Stein, and the Huang family provided funding. Three deans of the Stanford Graduate School of Education—Deborah Stipek, Claude Steele, and Dan Schwartz—advised and encouraged me. Many friends and associates reviewed the cases along the way, including Sandy Baba, Dianna Ballesteros, Angel Barrios, T. Berry Brazelton, Holly Elissa Bruno, Victor Carrion, Laura Carstensen, Parul Chandra, Susanne Denham, Martina Ebusugawa, Linda Egbeer, Todd Erickson, Yolanda Garcia, Ed Greene, Betsy Haehl, Ilene Hertz, Nancy Howe, Alice Li Mark, Gwen Morgan, Susan Muenchow, Julie Nicholson, Peckie Peters, Judy Shulman, Josh Sparrow, Jeanne Tsai, Nancy Verdtzabella, Valora Washington, Roger Weissberg, Marcy Whitebook, Jennifer Winters, Rosalie Whitlock, and Ed Zigler.

I began writing and researching this book as an individual with disabilities, unable to use my arms and hands to keyboard or write. So many individuals assisted me with transcribing my dictated documents and identifying and retrieving research studies and other documents, that they are too numerous to mention all of them by name. But several were especially helpful: I am particularly grateful to Debra Hine, Nancy Luong, Katie Clapper, and Angelina Garron.

I also want to thank my siblings: Pat Daly, Joe Daly, and Mary Daly (all current or retired university faculty), and Gerry Daly. Several dear friends—Chip Brienza, Judy Hagopian, Nazila Alasti, Leah Friedman, and the late Fran Eizenstat—consistently encouraged me.

My daughters and their husbands—Cara and Dave Barone and Tracy and Paul Frey—also supported me. My four grandchildren—Ryan, Lucia, Silas, and Reeves—gave me innumerable opportunities to observe the development of emotional and social intelligence.

Most of all, my dear husband and best friend, Phil Pizzo, believed in this project and in my ability to complete it, without wavering. He provided supports of all kinds—and the loving feedback that makes any intellectual activity a work of the heart as well as the head.

Introduction

with Teresa Gonczy O'Rourke

This book seeks to help instructors engage future and current early child-hood education teachers and leaders in a type of learning that will ulti-mately increase overall skills in children and adults, especially the growth of emotional and social intelligence. We see well-developed emotional and social intelligence as a route to greater life happiness and to school and oc-cupational success. The six in-depth teaching cases in this book are intended to ultimately provide a resource to early childhood leaders that can be used to further develop emotional intelligence in children and adults.

In this introduction, we explain why we think a professional develop-ment approach based on the use of teaching cases matters, how the cases might be used, and what both developmentally appropriate practice is and how the cases are grounded in it. Since these cases are intended to foster the development of emotional intelligence, we also offer a definition of this ability and discuss three major frameworks for describing the skills that comprise this kind of intelligence. Finally, we provide a summary of each case, while explaining the sources in the relevant literature that were used to develop the case, including the questions at the end of each case that are intended to guide discussion.

A PROFESSIONAL DEVELOPMENT APPROACH
BASED ON TEACHING CASES

The case method of instruction is a pedagogy that incorporates complex real-life narrative cases with in-depth discussions to bridge theoretical knowledge with practical experience. Many professional schools, includ-ing top-ranked law, business, and medical schools, use the case method to prepare their students for the types of situations they will face once they are in the workforce (Lynn, 1999). Some education schools that are ready-ing K–12 educators for the classroom have also blended the case method into their courses (Merseth, 1996), and a few short cases have been devel-oped in early childhood education (Rand & NAEYC, 2000). This casebook further develops the case method of instruction in early childhood education teacher preparation and professional development through a variety of in-depth cases on topics including aggression and problem solving, executive functioning and self-regulation, the child's experience of trauma, and early childhood leadership and administration.

What Are Teaching Cases?

Teaching cases are "complex educational instruments that appear in the form of narratives" (Wassermann, 1994, p. 3). Teaching cases tell a story with a setting, characters, and a conflict. This conflict often has multiple dilemmas and many nuances without an easy answer or resolution. The readers engage with the narrative in a very different way than they might read a textbook, empathizing with the characters and relating the story to their own experiences. However, a case is not only an interesting story to read, but a case is "a case of *something*, or an instance of a larger class" (Shulman, Whittaker, & Lew, 2002, p. xii). A case is an example of a common situation (or multiple common situations) and is connected to general principles, even if the particulars of the case are unique.

In this early childhood education casebook, the teaching cases are complex and hopefully compelling, research-based narratives written in a practitioner-friendly format that vividly describe practitioners working through challenging scenarios. These early childhood practitioners, including teachers, assistants, program directors, and other leaders, transform the challenges and crises into opportunities for further growth, especially in building social and emotional intelligence. This growth may happen for the children in the case, as well as for the practitioners who are working with the children and families.

The teaching cases in this casebook were developed and written by combining reviews of relevant research studies, public- and private-sector program guidance or "best practices," policy and site-based documents, and observations and in-depth interviews with early childhood practitioners. The purpose of developing the teaching cases this way is to create research-grounded narratives that are highly related to the workings of real early care and education programs.

An effective teaching case resonates with authenticity, including the struggles of practitioners. Students and faculty who read a case should recognize issues that they have experienced in actual early childhood programs—or if they have not yet had practical experience, that they hear others, in a discussion of the case, describe as familiar issues that arise in actual programs.

However, an effective teaching case also leaves some distance between the personal and professional experiences of those practitioners and experts, slightly disturbing the accustomed thought patterns and knowledge base of the readers. This perturbation provokes reflection in the readers, opening them to new insights. In the guided group discussion, healthy and even vigorous debate about a case ensues. Through this debate, the discussants develop an "inner portfolio" of strategies and approaches that may work well for them in their own programs. In addition, because the cases are rooted in actual experiences in the field, textured nuances emerge that could provide researchers conducting empirical studies with fresh hypotheses to test.

This combination of closeness and distance allows the discussants of the case to both recognize similarities and feel that the narrative reflects best practices. Sometimes the discussants might object to the high standards for practitioner behavior embodied in a best-practices case, as they may not have personally experienced or observed such behavior. This can provoke interesting discussions as the distance felt in reading about experiences they have not yet encountered encourages discussants to engage in more reflective inquiry about the many issues presented in a case.

A teaching case also leaves the solution or resolution to the portrayed scenario slightly incomplete or ambivalent, in order to stimulate thought, especially as discussants are encouraged to voice their opinions about other possible solutions to the dilemma. Following each narrative is a series of questions designed to inspire discussion, as well as reflection and self-inquiry. At the end of each case are research resources, organized around the issues that surfaced in the case, for those who want to dive deeper and learn more. In addition, the Recommended Reading section at the end of the book provide an extraordinary list of all the scholarly reading done by the author to prepare and interpret the classroom observations and interviews with teachers, leaders, and experts. This resource is for readers deeply interested in emotional intelligence or in any of the subtopics of the cases; it will allow them to quickly identify research, best practice guidance, and policy-relevant documents and resources, and to deepen their knowledge.

Why a Casebook for Early Childhood Teacher Education?

As mentioned above, the case method has long been used in professional schools (business, law, medicine) to give students the opportunity to delve into the practical application of the theories they are learning. Case pedagogy in K–12 teacher training has its roots as early as 1920, and it grew significantly in the 1980s and 1990s with many casebooks being published (Merseth, 1999). Despite the large influence of the case method in K–12 teacher education, early childhood teacher education and professional development has only recently seen a few instances of the case method being used (Angeli, 2004; Lee & Choi, 2008; Rand & NAEYC, 2000; Snyder & McWilliam, 2003). Typically the preservice and ongoing training that early learning teachers receive is not high-quality and is not aligned with what they need for the classroom (Gomez, Kagan, & Fox, 2015; Linder, Rembert, Simpson, & Ramey, 2016).

Early care and education is a critically important first step in children's education pathway (Yoshikawa et al., 2013), and we need early childhood professionals with strong skills and knowledge to teach in our classrooms (Institute of Medicine & National Research Council, 2015). Early childhood teachers and administrators deal with ambiguous situations every day where there is not one "right answer." Teaching can be thought of as improvising all day long, and even more so for early childhood teaching, as young children are more unpredictable and are more often engaged in free play as opposed to following a structured lesson plan. Early care and education teachers need to be nimble in their responses and to have a portfolio of ideas and strategies upon which to draw.

The case method of instruction can be highly beneficial for early childhood teacher preparation and training because it allows teachers to bridge research and practice with real-life scenarios, to connect their theoretical knowledge with practical application, to "relate theory-based ideas to predicaments of practice" (Gravett, de Beer, Odendaal-Kroon, & Merseth, 2017). Through reading, analyzing, and discussing cases, early childhood teachers can build skills in autonomous problem solving and decision-making (Barnett & Tyson, 1999). They can practice using evidence, recognizing patterns, and thinking reflectively and analytically. By discussing the cases with others, they improve their understanding of the case issues (Levin, 1995), understand multiple perspectives, test out their assumptions about practice (Shulman, 1992), and use metacognition (thinking about their thinking). Teachers can "clarify and question [their] personal beliefs/values through agreement and disagreement," possibly "alter[ing] previously held beliefs" (Lundeberg, 1999, p. 5). All of these habits of mind are needed by early care and education teachers to effectively deal with the many different challenges within the early childhood classroom.

How Should This Casebook Be Used?

The case method of instruction is very different from the typical higher education format of assigning a reading in a textbook and then lecturing about the topic area during class time. The case method requires more preparation on the part of the students as well as the professor. Case discussion is a key component of the case method, where "students learn not only from the teacher but from each other by bringing their collective experience to bear on the problem" (Schiano & Anderson, 2014, p. 2). Students often get the most out of the case from these large group discussions, hearing others' perspectives and ideas (Levin, 1999).

The case method begins with individual analysis of the dilemma. The written case should be thoroughly read and analyzed first by each student individually. The student might highlight sentences in the text and take notes to better keep track of the different aspects of the case. Some students find it helpful to write character bios so they better understand the multiple characters and their actions in the case. The professor can assign several (or all) of the questions, perhaps based on the curriculum topic area currently being studied. Students may be asked to record their answers to the questions, although the reading and the individual analysis are only the starting point for the case method.

Because cases can be complex with many moving parts and characters, many students get value out of forming small study groups to discuss the case and go over the questions before class time. If it's inconvenient for students to find time to discuss before class, professors may hold study group sessions at the beginning of class time. During these small study groups, students can go over their understanding of the case, asking the other students how they interpreted different actions and what they might have done differently in the situation. By working through the case with others, students deepen their understanding of the complex issues at play in these common situations within early childhood classrooms and agencies, realizing that there is rarely a "right" answer, but instead many ways to handle intricate dilemmas with children, parents, teachers, and leaders.

After individual reading and small-group analysis, the key aspect of the case method, the case discussion, happens during class time. The professor facilitates the case analysis discussion with the whole class. The case method works best with smaller class sizes (preferably less than 35 students), so that all students might have the chance to participate in the discussion. The professor will have notes about major points the class should cover, but the discussion is led mostly by the students and their thoughts about the case and the dilemmas within. Initially, the professor should focus on helping the students work with the issues in the case itself before the students bring in their experiences. While it may be tempting to just assign the case as a reading, professors and students will not reap the benefits of the case method without the case discussion.

While the case discussion is student-powered, preparing for the discussion is critical for professors. Facilitating a case discussion is a grand improvisation act that takes time to master. Some professors use "cold-calling," where the professor picks who will participate in the discussion next, and some professors "issue open invitations to participate and encourage" students (Lynn, 1999, p. 76). A strong case discussion often includes some of both—open invitations and cold-calling—to give students the chance to participate when they have something specific to say and to draw everyone into the discussion. Professors would do well to work to strike a balance that leaves students feeling safe but also engaged, where students can bring up aspects of the case that they want to understand better, but the professor also keeps the conversation on topic and focused on why this particular case was assigned to the students in the first place. The professor's questions might encourage students to reexamine their ideas about the case, call for students to analyze an idea, challenge students to generate new ideas, promote cognitive dissonance, or help students reflect and integrate their experiences (Wassermann, 1994). These questions are often followed by responses from multiple students, without evaluative comments in between, thus creating a large-scale discussion, rather than the question-and-answer cycle typical in higher education courses (Levin, 1995).

In planning out a preservice course using this casebook, the professor could use just one or two cases that focus on specific topics that should be covered—preschoolers learning to share, for example, or the development of self-regulation and executive function in children with challenging behaviors. Or a professor could design a whole course that revolves around all of the cases in this casebook. Because reading and analyzing a case requires a fair amount of time for both the students and the professor, having a new case every other class session, rather than every class session, is likely to work well. Other types of coursework, including more typical textbook readings, lectures, or even time in an early childhood classroom, can be interspersed with the cases to broaden students' understanding and help them connect the theoretical knowledge with the practical experience. The "Resources for Delving Deeper" section at the end of each case lists selected resources on relevant topic areas for the professor or students.

The cases in this casebook are designed for upper-division undergraduate and graduate-level students, as well as similarly skilled students in professional development or leadership classes. They are designed to be particularly relevant to the needs of students in well-supervised field experiences or those currently employed in programs. The cases would be informative both for students in early childhood education programs as well as for students in related programs, such as K–12 education, psychology, and education policy. While students who have already spent some time in an early childhood classroom might bring stories of similar dilemmas to the case discussion, those who have not yet been in the classroom also bring relevant and insightful experiences to the conversation, often getting others to think outside the typical way of "solving" problems in early childhood education.

In addition to the typical case method using prewritten cases such as the ones in this book, professors can extend the case method through giving small groups of students the task of creating their own cases. Creating a new case requires writing skills, but also observation, analysis, and metacognition. Students could develop a new case from their own experiences combined with their academic knowledge, or students could do research to write a real-life case. They could observe in a classroom, as well as interview teachers, administrators, parents, and children, to better understand the multiple perspectives and thus more fully describe a real situation. Engaging students in creating a case gives them additional perspectives into the many nuances of dilemmas within the early childhood education field.

DEVELOPMENTALLY APPROPRIATE PRACTICE

The early childhood field can, fortunately, look to developmentally appropriate practice, a comprehensive framework rooted in research about ways young children develop and learn and in what is known about early education approaches that are effective (Copple & Bredekamp, 2009). Designed with considerable input from the early childhood field, DAP is organized around three core considerations:

- Typical characteristics of child development and learning at each age and stage
- Each child's unique interest, abilities, and developmental progress
- The cultural values, expectations, and forces in children's families and communities that influence children's lives

First adopted as a framework in 1986 by NAEYC, DAP has guided the early care and education field as a "gold standard" of teaching practice ever since. NAEYC position statements about DAP have been periodically issued after considerable input from the field and on the basis of new knowledge generated by research. Some of the issues which DAP has tried to address include the following:

- Achievement gap between children from different income and ethnic backgrounds
- Accountability movement that has resulted in both early childhood learning standards at the state level and child's outcomes framework for Head Start
- Pressures on teachers and leaders in early childhood programs to produce more academic outcomes
- Importance of well-qualified teachers and good research-based curricular guidance that is needed by all teachers
- Value of intentional and respectful engagement with all kinds of families
- Significance of teaching approaches that emphasize the social and emotional development of young children along with their learning in the mathematics and literacy arenas

THE FOCUS ON EMOTIONAL INTELLIGENCE IN THIS CASEBOOK

What Is Emotional Intelligence?

Emotional intelligence is a set of skills that can be learned by both adults and children. These skills enable us to be aware of our own and others' feelings and to guide our thoughts and actions better by using that enhanced awareness and a set of related skills, which will be discussed below.

The first academic work developing the theory of emotional intelligence was done by Peter Salovey and Jack Mayer (1990). They were the first scholars to oppose the then-prevailing view that most emotions were inferior to reason and should be entirely avoided in personal and professional lives and de-emphasized in scholarly research on human development and behavior. Instead, they proposed that emotions provide information that could be used to enhance thought, rather than degrade it. Their definition of *emotional intelligence* has stood the test of time:

> We define E.I. [Emotional Intelligence] as the capacity to reason about emotions and of emotions to enhance thinking. It includes the abilities to accurately perceive emotions, to access and generate emotions so as to assist thought, to understand emotions and emotional knowledge, and to reflectively regulate emotions so as to promote emotional and intellectual growth. (Mayer, Salovey, & Caruso, 2004, p. 197)

The scholarly work by Salovey and Mayer was popularized by Daniel Goleman, then a science writer for the *New York Times*, in his best selling book, *Emotional Intelligence: Why It Can Matter More Than IQ* (1995). Goleman blended knowledge and insights from the fields of psychology and neuroscience, research, and best practices rooted in the application of these new scientific findings to actual programs serving human beings, including schools. Goleman then went on to write many more books and articles that informed the lay reader why emotional intelligence matters—for the work place (1998), for leadership (2004), and for attention and focus (2013). Along the way, Daniel Goleman began meeting with the Dalai Lama, who had long been interested in bringing together the Buddhist emphasis on understanding and training the mind—and its origins in millennia-old Buddhist scholarship about the mind—into greater connection with the emerging neuroscientific findings about the mind, including the power of both positive and destructive emotions (Goleman, 2003). Together, they collaborated in the further development of the Mind and Life Institute, a working group that brings together Buddhist scholars with neuroscientists and other social scientists (see www.mindandlife.org).

Goleman had also teamed up with Tim Shriver, a longtime activist in support of better educational opportunity for children, and Roger Weissberg, a developmental psychologist, to found the Collaborative for Academic, Social, and Emotional Learning (2017b).

CASEL was developed in 1994 with the goal of "establishing high-quality, evidence-based social and emotional learning (SEL) as an essential part of preschool through high school education" (2017a). Social and emotional learning is defined by CASEL as "the process through which children and adults acquire and effectively apply the knowledge, attitudes, and skills necessary to understand and manage emotions, set and achieve positive goals, feel and show empathy for others, establish and maintain positive relationships, and make responsible decisions" (2017e).

From its earliest days, CASEL sought to continually bring together leading social scientists and educators to create syntheses of the evidence for the positive impact of SEL on the academic, social, and emotional outcomes of children and youth. The evidence has been and continues to be quite persuasive. In a recent meta-analysis of 213 studies involving more than 270,000 students, those who participated in effective SEL programs displayed an 11-percentile point gain in academic achievement compared to students who did not participate (CASEL, 2017d).

In addition to synthesizing research about positive academic and other outcomes, CASEL has publicized exceptionally promising studies that show positive life outcomes from SEL programs, such as a 2015 study showing important outcomes in "education, employment, [reduced] criminal activity, [reduced] substance use and mental health" (American Enterprise Institute for Public Policy Research and the Brookings Institution, 2015).

CASEL also produces program guides for educational leaders and practitioners to use in implementing SEL programs throughout the country and the world. Although CASEL does try to address the research and best practice needs of preschool educators and leaders, the overwhelming majority of its excellent syntheses and inventories of research studies and programs focus on the K–12 grades. We note, however, that there are ratings for and great descriptions of a few well-known preschool-focused programs. These include High Scope (a curriculum originating in the Perry Preschool Project that emphasizes direct, hands-on child-centered learning); the Incredible Years (a program that successfully aims to prevent and treat young children's behavior problems); the Preschool Promoting Alternative Thinking Strategies (Preschool PATHS), a curriculum designed to assist preschool educators and counselors in helping young children develop "better self-control, self-esteem, emotional awareness, basic problem-solving skills, social skills, and friendships" (PATHS® Training, 2011); and the Tools of the Mind, a curriculum that helps preschool children "develop the cognitive, social–emotional, self-regulating and foundational academic skills they need to succeed in school and beyond" (Tools of the Mind, 2017).

These curricula all have proven track records in helping children develop greater emotional and social intelligence. CASEL has done a good service to the early childhood community by providing information about them. They have informed the writing of this casebook, which aims to introduce the reader to resources like this.

Frameworks for Emotional and Social Intelligence

Three major frameworks for understanding the essential elements of emotional intelligence informed the development of this casebook. They are the CASEL framework; the RULER framework developed by the Yale Center for Emotional Intelligence; and the Six Seconds framework. I discuss each of these briefly below.

The CASEL Framework. The CASEL framework uses five elements as essential skills for emotional intelligence:

- *Self-awareness.* The ability to accurately recognize one's emotions, thoughts, values, strengths, and limitations, with an understanding of how these influence behavior and a grounded self-confidence, optimistic outlook, and mindset that skills can be grown.
- *Self-management.* The ability to control one's emotions, thoughts and behaviors, and impulses, managing stress and motivating oneself effectively. Being able to set and work toward personal and academic goals is part of self-management.
- *Social awareness.* The ability to see situations from the perspective of others, including culturally diverse individuals. Being able to understand social and ethical behavioral standards is also part of the overall skill of social awareness.
- *Relationship skills.* The ability to establish and maintain good relationships with diverse individuals and groups, but also the ability to "resist inappropriate social pressure, negotiate conflict constructively, and seek and offer help when needed."
- *Responsible decision making.* The ability to make good choices about behavior, grounded in ethical standards, while taking into account safety concerns, social norms, and appraisal of the consequences of actions on the well-being of oneself and others. (CASEL, 2017c)

The RULER Framework. RULER is an acronym for a framework developed by Marc Brachett of Yale University, who was mentored by Peter Salovey and Jack Mayer. The letters in the acronym represent the five elements of the framework:

Recognizing emotions in self and others
Understanding the causes and consequences of emotions
Labeling emotions accurately
Expressing emotions appropriately
Regulating emotions effectively (Nathanson, Rivers, Flynn, & Brackett, 2016).

The Six Seconds Framework. Finally, the Six Seconds framework is intended to help individuals become "more aware (noticing what you do), more intentional (doing what you mean), and more purposeful (doing it for a reason)" (Freedman, 2012, para. 3).

Karen Stone McCown and Anabel Jensen, who have also been deeply involved in the development of two widely recognized schools for the gifted and talented that emphasize SEL—Nueva School and Synapse School—developed this framework. Six Seconds encompasses three essential elements and eight competencies. The first element is to Know Yourself. "When you know yourself," says Joshua Freedman (2012), the Executive Director of Six Seconds, "you know your strengths and challenges, you know what you are doing, what you want and what you want to change" (para. 7). The second element is to Choose Yourself. According to Freedman, choosing yourself shows you how to take action, how to influence yourself and others. Finally, the third element is to Give Yourself. Joshua Freedman describes this as a skill that, with clarity and energy, allows one to "stay focused as to why to respond a certain way, why to move in a new direction and why others should come on board" (para. 9).

The eight competencies—measured by the Six Seconds Emotional Intelligence Assessment—include the following skills:

1. Enhancing emotional literacy
2. Recognizing patterns (in reactions and behaviors)
3. Applying consequential thinking (evaluating the costs and benefits of one's choices)
4. Navigating emotions
5. Engaging intrinsic motivation
6. Exercising optimism
7. Increasing empathy
8. Pursuing noble goals

The Six Seconds framework is used in corporations and diverse adult-oriented organizations as well as schools.

Peggy consciously used one or more of these thoughtful and well-developed frameworks as one element in constructing the challenges and opportunities for growth in the behaviors of both adults and children in the cases.

THE CASES IN THIS CASEBOOK

The cases in this casebook evolved from many hours of classroom and leadership-meeting observations, extensive reviews of related research, interviews with practitioners and leaders, and content analysis of documents relevant to the classroom or organization. The issues and topics were selected on the basis of their importance to the optimal development of children in early care and education programs—and their relevance to contemporary issues that beset early childhood programs. The cases are divided into two Parts. In Part I, Cases 1–4 focus on teacher–child interaction and take up the issues of linguistic and cultural diversity, challenging behaviors and careful assessment of the causes for these behaviors, and trauma experienced by young children who have endured child abuse. In Part II, Cases 5–6 turn to early childhood leaders and explore the issues of exceptionally low wages for the early childhood workforce and the resulting severe challenges involved in recruiting and sustaining a qualified cadre of teachers in early childhood programs.

We want to note that all the teaching cases are drawn from classroom observations of best practices in three different early childhood program sites. But none of the situations described in these cases can be attributable to any one program. They are composites that do not describe individual practice in just one particular program. A brief summary of each case follows here so that instructors (or individual readers) using the casebook can more easily select the cases they want to use.

Part I. Cases on Teacher–Child Interaction

Case 1. Tomas, Arthur, and Sharing: Resolving Conflicts. "Tomas, Arthur, and Sharing" is a case designed to illustrate best practices that teachers might use to resolve conflicts over sharing, to encourage the development of empathy, and teach children how to respond to an early form of bullying behavior. The case shows teachers encouraging children to think about what constitutes a "turn" in taking turns, instead of resorting to the device of using a timer, for example, to allocate the number of minutes that each "turn" might take. This encourages the development of higher order and conceptual thinking in children.

In developing this case, Peggy drew from the excellent research of Susanne Denham (2006) illustrating the emotional development of young children and showing that "persistent persuasion" is the most effective approach in helping children learn to negotiate conflict and to problem share.

Case 2. Ming: A Mystery Story for Teachers and Student Teachers. This case focuses on a child who almost never interacts with teachers or children. The teachers struggle to decide whether Ming is a highly reserved child, a Chinese-speaking child in the very early stages of English language acquisition, or a child adhering to cultural guidance from home. They also struggle with engaging Ming's caregiver grandparents, who speak Mandarin but not English, and his very busy parents, who do speak English but are very hard to reach because of their work and study schedules. Cultural misunderstandings arise and the teachers try to problem-solve around those.

In writing this case, Peggy drew heavily from the research of Jerome Kagan about children with reserved temperament; from the work of the National Association for the Education of Young Children in promoting the importance of the awareness of cultural and linguistic diversity through both developmentally appropriate practice and key position statements; from the work of the California Department of Education in providing program guidance throughout the state on best practices in educatory preschool English learners; from the research of Jeanne Tsai in documenting the unique perspectives of Asian American and Asian children on happiness and other emotions (Tsai, 2007; Tsai, Louie, Chen, & Uchida, 2007; Tsai, Miao, Seppala, Fung, & Yeung, 2007); and from Professor Tsai's advice to Peggy about the types of cultural guidance that Chinese American preschool children would receive at home about the proper behavior at school (personal communication, March 16, 2012). Both Jeanne Tsai and Sandy Baba, cofounder of the NAEYC Asian Interest Forum (personal communication, April 9, 2012), helped Peggy understand the ways in which Chinese parents and grandparents would be likely to understand the proper relationship between home and school—that home visits, for example, can be highly alarming because in Chinese culture they would not take place unless the child had behaved quite badly. Since the case also deals with the issue of family engagement, Peggy used the framework developed by the National Technical Assistance Center on Parent, Family, and Community Engagement housed at Brazelton Touchpoints Center and Boston Children's Hospital at Harvard University.

Case 3. Sky-High Energy in Classroom Five. This case addresses a supremely challenging scenario for both teachers and teaching assistants: multiple children with very emotionally intense, highly active temperaments. Elijah and Daniel, 4-year-old African American twins, continually energize each other throughout the day, stimulating one another to rise to higher and higher levels of emotional intensity and activity. Teachers struggle to keep up with them, while also attending to the care and educational needs of all the other children in the classroom. Feeling overwhelmed, the teaching team approaches the director, arguing that the boys will have to be expelled from the school, as they are simply too much to handle. The director of the early care and education center encourages the teachers to pause and reflect, and to co-develop with her some classroom and family engagement strategies that are likely to help the boys better manage their intense, impulsive behavior. In addition, she works with the teachers and the family to arrange for a comprehensive evaluation of both boys. The results of the evaluation are both predictable beforehand—and somewhat surprising.

This case illustrates the dilemmas experienced by the teachers who love the very active, intense children in their care, but feel utterly unable to help them develop behaviors that are more informed by the brain's capacity for self-regulation and executive function.

In writing this case, Peggy and her coauthors, Teresa Gonczy O'Rourke and Ed Greene, used the resources on executive function and self-regulation developed by the Center on the Developing Child at Harvard University (2015). We also drew from the book *Tools of the Mind* by Elena Bodrova and Deborah Leong (2007), who have used the theories of Vygotsky (1978) on the social and cultural forces that shape learning to develop a curriculum that helps children develop executive function and self-regulation skills. In addition, we used the excellent book, *Challenging Behavior in Young Children* (2017) by Barbara Kaiser and Judy Sklar Rasminsky—a resource full of research summaries and descriptions of best practices that are likely to be very helpful to teachers. The books of Marilou Hyson—on the emotional development of young children (2004) and on enthusiastic and engaged learners (2008)—were also great resources for this case.

Finally, since we chose to craft a case that would raise the policy-relevant issues of expulsion and of bias—issues predominantly affecting boys of color, particularly African American boys—we drew on the research of Oscar Barbarin and colleagues (Barbarin & Crawford, 2006; Barbarin, Murry, Tolan, & Graham, 2016) on the issues confronting the healthy development of boys of color. We also turned to the research of Walter Gilliam at Yale University on implicit bias and on expulsion (Gilliam, 2005; Gilliam & Shahar, 2006).

Case 4. Roberto and Maria: Two Children Dealing with Trauma. This case focuses on two children who have been physically and emotionally abused. Roberto, stuck in painful fears and memories, repeats certain behaviors over and over again in ways that call forth great compassion in his teacher, who successfully reclaims him from his traumatized state. His aggression toward other children is easily triggered, especially by Maria, who has also been abused. Working together as a team, the teachers and the program director engage the families of both children, despite having to report the abuse to the authorities. The relationship with Roberto's mother is significantly challenged, however, by her efforts to violate the court-mandated restraining order, which forbids her showing up at Roberto's care and education program. The case illustrates the teacher's dilemmas involved in trying to maintain good working relationships with parents who have been abusive, especially when court orders must be enforced. With much effort, sometimes painful uncertainties, and patience, the team's work results in substantial resolution of the trauma and significantly less challenging behaviors in the children.

Since this case also focuses on inadequate compensation for teachers as a central challenge to effective early childhood education leadership, I also drew on the research of Marcy Whitebook and her colleagues (2014) at the Center for the Study of Early Child Care Employment at the University of California at Berkeley. The position papers of the National Association for the Education of Young Children on early childhood teaching as a profession also proved helpful (2012b, n.d.).

Since the case also deals with the issue of family engagement, Peggy used the framework for family engagement developed by the National Center on Parent, Family, and Community Engagement (eclkc.ohs.acf.hhs.gov/about-us/article/national-center-parent-family-community-engagement-ncpfce).

In developing this case, Peggy turned to overviews of trauma such as the most recent comprehensive reports (National Academy of Sciences, 2008), and the excellent framework for intervention when trauma has occurred based on promoting attachment, self-regulation and competency, developed by Kinniburgh, Blaustein, and Spinazzola (2005). The National Child Traumatic Stress Network (2008) also proved to be an excellent resource. To understand the impact of trauma, both on the severely abused child in the case, Roberto, and on potentially his mother, during her childhood, Peggy used the Adverse Childhood Experience (ACE) study (Center for Disease Control and Prevention, 2016), with its investigation of the long-term cumulative negative impact of multiple adverse experiences on life outcomes. In understanding better how to help traumatized children, Peggy used the work of Alicia Lieberman (Chu & Lieberman, 2010; Lieberman, 1993), an internationally recognized expert; the comprehensive report produced by the Massachusetts Advocates for Children (Cole et al., 2005); and the excellent book *Trauma-Sensitive Schools* (Craig, 2016).

Part II. Cases on Early Childhood Leadership

Case 5. Coming to Ground: The Leaders of All Our Children Head Start Agency Visit a Local Center With Problems. In this case, recent child injuries at a Head Start center prompt agency leaders, Yolanda Garcia and Sahara Alexis, to pay a visit to the site. These leaders seek to promote both better health and safety measures at the center as well as higher educational quality. They also want to foster promising opportunities for closer collaboration with the public school with which this center shares a location. The visit is fraught with tension. The stakes are high because a significant licensing violation could lead to the center's license being revoked. This would jeopardize the federal funding of the entire 35 centers that comprise the All Our Children Head Start Agency.

The program director of this center, Helen, is well trained to the bachelor's degree level in child development, but has not been trained in program administration and has not had extensive experience in the classroom. So as a new untrained administrator, she confronts the chronic problem of early childhood center administration: recruiting both teachers and substitute teachers when compensation is very low. Problems in Helen's personal life have also recently distracted her from her job responsibilities.

Leaders Yolanda and Sahara struggle with some basic leadership issues of balance: stay at their desks using computerized monitoring information or leave their offices to go on site; focus on investigating problems versus seizing the opportunity of a personal visit to also promote new initiatives; unconditionally support a valued staff person who is also a friend or courageously inform her of possible placement on unpaid administrative leave because of the high-stakes threat of a licensing revocation.

In developing this case, I drew on the research-based best practices that are embedded in several streams: (1) literature on leadership; (2) program guidance on excellent health and safety related practices in early childhood programs; (3) some essential leadership-related elements of the Head Start Program Performance Standards, the core requirements defining quality in Head Start programs (U.S. Department of Health and Human Services, Administration for Children and Families, 2017); (4) the rating scales that leaders in early care and education programs must use, which are linked to obtaining and preserving funding.

There are several different types of literature in the field of leadership that are relevant to this case, but I especially relied on the work of Holly Elisa Bruno (2008, 2012), who has long written about leadership, specifically in early childhood programs. I also turned to the excellent portrayal of early childhood leadership in *The New Early Childhood Professional* by Valora Washington and colleagues (2015), as well as Stacey Goffin's analysis of what is needed to successfully professionalize the early childhood field in *Professionalizing Early Childhood Education as a Field of Practice* (2015). The literature in the broader field of leadership in general—especially work that documents the best practices in emotionally intelligent leadership, such as the book *Primal Leadership* (2002) by Daniel Goleman and his colleagues—proved particularly helpful. Finally, Jim Collins (2005) provides a valuable description of leadership issues specific to the nonprofit sector.

The overarching framework for the emotional and social intelligence skills that are used by the leaders depicted in this case continues to be that developed by CASEL (2017c) with its five key elements of self-awareness, self-management or self-regulation, social awareness, relationship skills, and responsible decision making.

Case 6. Crises and Compassion: The Leaders of All Our Children Head Start Agency Use Emotional and Social Intelligence to Navigate Through Challenges. This case is addressed to the leadership of large agencies (e.g., large Head Start grantees including those working hard to collaborate with school districts or pre-K programs in large school districts). It portrays leaders at a full-day leadership retreat struggling to make a difficult decision about accepting more funding (which means accepting an additional layer of quality assurance requirements, when they already have multiple layers they are complying with). Some of the leaders argue forcefully that the funds for professional development should be turned back, unless the funding agency agrees that these funds could be spent on increased wages for teachers—central to improving quality. This dilemma informs the entire case. As the leaders struggle with this dilemma, a typical, but highly challenging, crisis surfaces. Due to the chronically low compensation for teaching staff, the agency has been dealing with a severe problem of shortages of teachers and the resulting struggle to recruit substitutes. But today, there are not enough substitutes, and so the leaders must decide who can even stay at this biannual leadership retreat, since some leaders with classroom experience must leave this important discussion in order to cover the classrooms that are lacking sufficient teachers.

Since this case also focuses on inadequate compensation for teachers as a central challenge to effective early childhood education leadership, Peggy drew on the research of Marcy Whitebook and her colleagues (2014) at the Center for the Study of Child Care Employment at the University of California at Berkeley.

CONCLUSION

We hope that the reader will come to the end of this Introduction with a better understanding of the case-based approach to the preparation and ongoing professional development of teachers and leaders, of the frameworks and research that influenced the development of the cases in this book, and of the cases themselves.

Part I

CASES ON TEACHER-CHILD INTERACTION

Tomas, Arthur, and Sharing
Resolving Conflicts

Three Corners Preschool is an early care and education program, with both outdoor and indoor play areas, serving 32 children aged 3 and 4 in each classroom. Well-organized indoor and outdoor activities are guided by a 4-member teaching team in each classroom, led by teachers with extensive experience. Two teachers have BA degrees and one (the lead teacher) has both an MA and long-term experience. The lead teacher also serves as a mentor teacher to the other teachers. In addition, there is one student teacher on the team.

In this case, teacher Lucia is a 1st-year teacher who has just completed her BA. Teacher Susan has a BA and 15 years of teaching experience.

The lead teacher and several of the other teachers believe strongly in a philosophy termed the "Competence Model" (P. Peters, personal communication, April 2012). They approach children with a belief in children's inherent strengths and positive intentions—and they feel that with this approach children will develop a stronger belief in themselves and particularly in their capacity to handle challenging situations or behaviors. They also strongly prefer to use reasoning and problem solving among the children as the best long-term solutions for helping children learn how to manage conflicts among themselves.

"MY TURN!" shouted Tomas, leaping over two carefully dug canyons full of water in the sand play area. "*My* turn now! *Compartimos* (*We share*)." Tomas grasps the long, green garden hose gripped tightly by Arthur in the sand play area of Three Corners Preschool.

Pulling vigorously, Tomas grabs the hose away from Arthur, who has been contentedly filling the canyons with water from the garden hose hooked up to the sand play area. "NO, NO, NO!" cries Arthur, resisting Tomas's efforts with all his 4-year-old strength. "NOT time yet!" Teacher Lucia crouches down, puts an arm around each boy's shoulder, and looks first at Arthur and then Tomas, directly in the eye.

"Both of you want to play with the garden hose right now, Tomas and Arthur. So, we have a problem to solve," she says firmly but kindly. "Arthur, you have been playing with the hose for a long time, and now your friend Tomas wants to have a turn."

"No," says Arthur, shaking his blond mop of curly hair. "I don't want to," he says, but a little less vigorously as his eyes lock with Lucia's. She smiles at him, "Well, how can we make sure that both of you get to play with the hose? How many turns should each friend have? Any ideas?"

"Yes," cries Arthur, excitedly, "I want a hundred turns!"

"I want a hundred turns, too!" says Tomas emphatically.

Lucia smiles at each of them. "One hundred turns! My, that is many, many turns. Can we come up with another idea? Is one hundred turns going to work really well for each of you? What do you think will be fair?"

"Okay, maybe 20 turns," says Tomas, eyeing the garden hose enviously, "but it is my turn now."

"Well," says teacher Lucia, "right now we are working on the problem of how many turns each of you should have. When we solve that problem, then we will work on whose turn comes next." Arthur, who has a close relationship with teacher Lucia, has been looking closely at her face as she speaks. "I think it should be 10 turns," he says, glancing briefly from Lucia's face over to Tomas and back. "Then we can both have enough turns."

"Well, Tomas," says teacher Lucia, drawing him a little closer to her, "What do you think about 10 turns?"

"I want it to be more, and I want to go next. Arthur had the hose for 50, a hundred turns, and it's my turn now."

"*No!*" says Arthur firmly, "ten turns is right." Now he turns directly to Tomas. "If you take 10 turns and I take 10 turns, then you won't have to wait too long and I won't have to wait too long. That's fair."

Lucia interjects, "I think we may have solved the problem. You, Tomas, will have 10 turns and then you, Arthur, will have 10 turns. How does this sound, friends?"

"No, no, no!" says Arthur, stamping his feet and giving teacher Lucia a betrayed look. "It's *still* my turn. I only had one turn. I should have more turns before it is Tomas's turn."

Teacher Lucia draws Arthur a little closer to her and shifts her weight on her feet as she stays crouching so that she can look each of the boys directly in their eyes. "Arthur, you played with the garden hose for a long time, ever since we finished snack and came outside. Tomas needs to play now, because pretty soon it will be time to go in to listen to a story and sing some songs."

"No, I *want* it," says Arthur. "It's not fair. My turn was too short. Ten turns and then I'll give it to Tomas."

"No," says Tomas, "My turn now"—and he makes a grab for the hose, which is now lying on the ground.

Lucia thinks to herself, "I remember reading in the book by Denham and Burton [2003, pp. 80–83] about the importance of the use of 'persistent persuasion' as a guidance technique in situations like this. I think this is what I am doing right now, but I wish I had more specific ideas about what to do next!" Then she remembers something she had heard the lead teacher say last month: "You have to just keep talking and keep solving the problem with them and eventually they will come up with a solution that everybody finds fair. It's time-consuming, but it's worth it. They feel good about the solution—and about the problem-solving process. And they gain skills they can build on the next time a "sharing" issue arises. And so conflicts around sharing will be fewer because the children will have skills to draw from and confidence that they can use these skills to work out agreements to share."

Turning to Arthur, teacher Lucia says, "What's *your* idea, Arthur? You did play with the garden hose and now Tomas wants to play. What's your plan about how to make this fair?"

"Five turns," he mutters, turning his eyes to the ground. "Tomas can have it for five turns, and then it's *mine*."

"Tomas?" says teacher Lucia, "what do you think?"

"Okay," he says, happily grabbing the garden hose and smiling at both Lucia and Arthur. "My turn!" Then he turns to Arthur, "Five turns, Arthur, and then it will be your turn."

Teacher Lucia says, "Do you have a plan, Arthur and Tomas, for what you think makes for one turn?"

Arthur points to a small bucket and says, "Tomas can fill that bucket up and dump the water in the canyon that we are making. That will be one turn."

Tomas shakes his head vigorously and points to a larger bucket, saying, "Look, Arthur, if I fill up the bigger bucket for each turn, then when your five turns come, you will have bigger buckets to fill yourself."

Looking each of the boys in their eyes, teacher Lucia says, "Is this a plan that is okay with the both of you?" Arthur, still eyeing the garden hose, grumbles assent. Teacher Lucia says, "You boys have tried hard to solve this problem. You thought and thought, and you talked and talked about it, and you came up with a plan to solve the problem."

"In the meantime, Arthur," says teacher Lucia, "while Tomas is having his turns with the hose, you could go get one of those big shovels over there and dig another really deep canyon. Then when it *is* your turn, you will be able to fill it with *more* water." Arthur mutters, "Okay," and heads toward the table against which the long-handled plastic shovels are stacked. But as he does so, he kicks over buckets of sand that three little girls—Kim, Hillary, and Maria—had been carefully filling.

The three girls start to cry, and teacher Lucia begins to head toward Arthur and the girls just as Tomas, having grabbed the hose, waves it around gleefully, shouting, "*Me toca a mí!* My turn!" With the hose, he showers the three little girls whose buckets of sand have just been kicked over by Arthur. Their tears of protest intensify.

Teacher Lucia thinks, "Where do I go first? Arthur? Kim, Hillary, and Maria? Or Tomas? It's hard to know!"

The lead teacher had recently suggested that should Lucia feel overwhelmed, she ought to send a signal to the "floater teacher" for the day. Each classroom session has one teacher assigned to be the "floater," who can move to an area where emotions are running high and social behavior is beginning to become a challenge. So Lucia looks hastily up and sees the very experienced teacher Susan and waves to her. Susan leaves the outdoor patio area and begins to move rapidly toward Lucia.

Lucia decides to work with Tomas first, reasoning that Arthur has probably given voice (or leg) to his frustrations and will move on toward the shovels, and the girls will be wet again unless she focuses on Tomas. Kneeling down, she takes each of Tomas's shoulders gently in her hands and brings his face to her own, looking right in his eyes. She knows that Tomas is a dual-language learner. His English skills are fairly good—since this is his 2nd year in English-speaking preschool—but when he gets excited it is hard for him to speak or fully understand any language other than his home language, Spanish. Fortunately, Lucia can speak and understand some phrases in Spanish.

"*Nada mas, Tomas. Mira sus amigas. Son muy tristes* (No more, Tomas. Look at your friends. They're very sad)." Tomas looks back at Lucia, as she gently removes the hose from his grasp and points it downward into the canyon. At first his eyes follow the hose, where his own goal lies: filling up that canyon with plenty of water from the hose. But teacher Lucia persists, "*Mira las caras de sus amigas, Kim, Hillary, y Maria* (Look at the faces of your friends, Kim, Hillary, and Maria)." Tomas, still holding the hose, now looks over at the girls.

Teacher Lucia reflects, "Perhaps this is what the other teachers must mean by 'competency modeling'—I do believe that Tomas *can* develop more empathy for these girls and that he will act on that empathy."

Teacher Susan has now reached the three girls and, kneeling down, puts her arms around all three and talks to them quietly. Tomas looks more carefully at the three girls; Hillary, also an active child, is one of his favorite playmates. "I'm sorry," says Tomas. Arthur looks up from his sand shoveling, but doesn't say anything.

Teacher Susan says to each of the girls, "What would you like to say to Tomas and Arthur?" She positions herself to look each of the girls in the eyes, encouraging them. "Is there something you would like to say to them?"

"Yes!" says Hillary, "Don't kick over our buckets, Arthur, we just finished filling them with sand. That's not fair." Teacher Susan says, "It's good to tell both Arthur *and* Tomas how you feel about what happened." Hillary looks at Tomas and says, "Don't *do* that with the hose, Tomas. It made me feel wet and cold, and I *don't* like that!" Maria and Kim, who are quieter children, nod their heads in assent.

With a little gentle hug from teacher Susan, all three girls retreat to another part of the sand area with their empty buckets, to begin filling them up again. Accompanying them, teacher Susan says, "You can tell Tomas or *anyone* when they do something you don't like. You can say: 'I *don't* like that, please *don't* do that again!'" Two of the girls look up at her as she walks with them, clearly listening. Kim seems more absorbed in managing her two buckets. Teacher Susan wonders how she can capture Kim's attention for this important communication. Why is Kim not responding now?

QUESTIONS FOR DISCUSSION

1. One way of understanding the children's behavior in this case is through the lens of their struggles around certain areas of preschool social and emotional competence. The Collaborative for Academic, Social, and Emotional Learning and Susanne Denham (Denham & Weissberg, 2003) define the following skills as hallmarks of preschool social and emotional competence:

    • Self-awareness
    • Social awareness
    • Self-management or self-regulation
    • Relationship management
    • Problem solving leading toward eventual responsible decision making

    Using this CASEL lens, what are the social and emotional issues that this case focuses on? Does it raise issues (and potential solutions to problem behavior) in each of the five CASEL areas, defined as hallmarks of social and emotional competence? If you agree that some of these five areas are addressed, which ones are they? Which ones are not?

2. In most preschool play yards, behavioral issues arise that need skilled teacher–child interaction in order to help the children develop better social and emotional skills and therefore better attention and behavior. From your vantage point, what are the general behavioral issues that this case addresses? Develop a list of issues related to the children's behavior, then draw up a list of issues related to the teacher's behavior. Why do *you* think these are issues?

3. Teacher Lucia interacts with Tomas and Arthur with a number of strategies to help them learn to share. She does the following:

    • Crouches down to be able to look each child directly in the eyes, and puts a gentle arm around each boy's shoulder
    • Identifies that there is a problem for the boys to solve and briefly describes the problem
    • Patiently and persistently asks the boys to propose ideas for solving

the problem and maintains as much eye contact as possible as she does so

- Repeatedly reminds the boys that there is a problem to solve and gently challenges each of them to talk through a strategy for sharing—in this case, a plan for how many turns is fair for each child to have

Do you see any other strategies that teacher Lucia uses in this particular case?

4. How would you interact with children when they refuse to share or take turns? Kick apart a structure that another child or group of children have made? How would this kind of interaction with children help them develop the social and emotional competencies listed above?

5. Do you think that Tomas and Arthur, having negotiated with the teacher an agreement that each boy will have five turns with the garden hose, are likely to be fair and reasonable with each other in deciding when each boy's five turns are up and it's time for the other one to have his five turns? Please support your opinion with your own experience and your own reading thus far in the child development and early childhood education literature. (For relevant reading, see Denham & Burton, 2003.)

6. Some would argue that a timer or a watch —a concrete object giving the children concrete evidence of how long a "turn" should last—would be necessary in a situation like this. What is your opinion? Support your ideas with analysis of what the use of concrete objects like this does in the long term for the children's development of self-regulation—as well as in the short term. If you think that "persistent persuasion" without the use of a concrete object is a better strategy for the development of long-term self-regulation, please give your reasons why.

7. What are the advantages and disadvantages of how teacher Lucia interacted with Tomas and Arthur? What would be other ways of interacting? Develop a list of alternative strategies and the advantages and disadvantages of each.

8. Teacher Susan responds to and guides Kim, Hillary, and Maria, the three distressed girls, by doing the following things:

- Kneeling down to put her arms around all three girls and talk to them quietly
- Continuing to position herself to look each of the girls in the eye
- Directly asking the girls what they would like to say to each boy
- Encouraging them to put their feelings into words and speak to each boy

- Urging them with her own positive words to speak up for themselves any time someone does something they don't like

Are there any other strategies that teacher Susan uses with the three girls? What are the advantages and disadvantages of each of the approaches that teacher Susan uses?

9. What strategies would *you* use to help the girls? Why? What would be some alternatives? How would this kind of interaction with children help them develop the social and emotional competencies listed above?

10. Do you think that Tomas, Arthur, Hillary, Kim, and Maria *are* learning some of the CASEL skills listed above? Why or why not?

11. Does teacher Lucia's passing familiarity with some words and phrases in Spanish make a difference for Tomas? Describe why (or why not) you think this is so. Should preschool teachers be required to learn at least some parts of another language as part of their professional development?

RESOURCES FOR DELVING DEEPER

The Development of Social and Emotional Competence in Young Children

Copple, C., & Bredekamp, S. (2009) *Developmentally appropriate practice in early childhood programs serving children from birth through age 8* (3rd ed., pp. 33–53, 119–129, 149–187). Washington, DC: National Association for the Education of Young Children.

California Department of Education, Child Development Division. (2008). *California preschool learning foundations* (Vol. 1). Sacramento: California Department of Education. (See especially the section on social and emotional development).

Denham, S. A. (1998). *Emotional development in young children.* New York, NY: Guilford Press.

Denham, S. A., & Burton, R. (2003). *Social and emotional prevention and intervention programming for preschoolers.* New York, NY: Kluwer Academic/Plenum.

Denham, S. A., & Weissberg, R. P. (2003). Social–emotional learning in early childhood: What we know and where to go from here. In E. Cheesebrough, P. King, T. P. Gullotta, & M. Bloom (Eds.), *A blueprint for the promotion of prosocial behavior in early childhood* (pp.13-50). New York, NY: Kluwer Academic/Plenum.

The Importance of Cultural and Linguistic Sensitivity in Teaching

Chang, F., Crawford, G., Early, D., Bryant, D., Howes, C., Margaret, B., . . . Pianta, R. C. (2007). Spanish-speaking children's social and language development in pre-kindergarten classrooms. *Early Education and Development, 18*(2), 243–269. doi:10.1080/10409280701282959

Day, C. B. (2006). Leveraging diversity to benefit children's social–emotional development and school readiness. In B. T. Bowman & E. Moore (Eds.), *School readiness and social–emotional development: Perspectives on cultural diversity* (pp. 23–32). Washington, DC: National Black Child Development Institute.

Espinosa, L. M. (2007). English-language learners as they enter school. In R. C. Pianta, M. J. Cox, & K. L. Snow (Eds.), *School readiness and the transition to kindergarten in the era of accountability* (pp. 175–198). Baltimore, MD: Paul H. Brookes.

Ming

A Mystery Story for
Teachers and Student Teachers

First Street Preschool is a NAEYC-accredited early care and education program in a working-class suburb wedged between a rural farmland area and a changing industrial area. The nearest large city is about an hour and a half away. The modestly sized outdoor and indoor play areas serve 18 children aged 3 and 4 in each of two classrooms. One lead teacher, Ranjita, and one teacher, Eduardo, staff Classroom 1. Ranjita is close to completing her BA degree and has had 15 years of experience at First Street Preschool. Eduardo, who has completed his AA degree and is working on coursework toward his bachelor's degree, has had 10 years of experience at the school. This semester, teachers Ranjita and Eduardo are joined by Anita, a student teacher from a 4-year state college located about 45 minutes away. This preschool serves a diverse community composed primarily of Latino, African American, East Indian, and Vietnamese families. However, there is only one Chinese family. Ming's family is an extended family composed of two grandparents, their two adult children and spouses, and five grandchildren. Ranjita speaks English, Hindi, and some Vietnamese. Eduardo speaks English, Spanish, and some Vietnamese, which he is learning from one of the parents who frequently volunteers in the classroom.

"I *cannot* believe it's the same child! Were we wrong about him?" Lead teacher Ranjita pulls her gaze away from Ming where he sits talking quietly to student teacher Anita, who joined the classroom 3 weeks ago for a semester of supervised teaching. Teacher Ranjita searches the face of her long-time coworker, teacher Eduardo.

Glancing at 4-year-old Ming, teacher Eduardo explains, "Amazing! For his whole 1st year here I thought we had a really shy and reserved child. Now look at what's happening. Is there something we should have done differently?"

Both teachers are briefly studying a short, sturdy child, who is talking with the new student teacher, Anita, as they make paper hats together at one of the art tables.

"This will have to wait till later," says Ranjita. "Looks to me like there are quite a few children in the swing and slide area, and I'd better get over there right away." Eduardo says, "I'm needed inside," and turns back to go inside the classroom. Both teachers agree to talk later, with student teacher Anita, at naptime, when things will be quiet at this all-day preschool.

Ming had entered this classroom at First Street Preschool last year, when he was just 3 years old. He has come every day to this full-year preschool for 16 months. For the first twelve months, he almost never spoke to any of the children and rarely interacted with a teacher. He scarcely ever smiled and typically wore a worried look on his face. Entering the classroom each morning with one of his grandparents (who spoke Chinese but not English) Ming would cling to his grandparent for quite a while. His grandparent would hold him close and talk quietly into his ear in Chinese. No one else in the classroom (or in the preschool) spoke Chinese.

Ming had participated in group child care before, but in another neighborhood about two hours away where many more Chinese families resided. Teachers Ranjita and Eduardo were not able to find out much about either his previous experience or his home life. From the preschool's director (who also doubled as a lead teacher in Classroom 2) they had learned that Ming's parents had immigrated here almost five years ago from China when his mother became pregnant with Ming. He does have a brother about four years older and a sister who had just recently celebrated her first birthday. He also has two school-age cousins living in an apartment down the street. His grandparents care for him and his siblings most of the time, and his cousins before and after school. His parents work during the day and go to school at night and part of the weekends, trying to improve their English and pursue degrees that would increase their earnings potential. They had recently moved to this neighborhood in order to be closer to the grandparents.

Once he had reluctantly said good-bye to his grandparent, Ming would head straight to the block-building area. Every day Ming would use all his free playtime to build block constructions: first towers and then houses with large walls around them.

In the block area, he lifted each block carefully and patted it into place with precise and careful gestures. Looking up from time to time, he would anxiously scan the children in the classroom. He built his block structures close to the wall, always leaving room for him to position himself between his block buildings and the wall. In warmer weather when the large hollow blocks were moved to the outside patio, he would quickly move to that area and stay there. As the other children played joyously and rambunctiously around him, Ming would look up from time to time and cautiously survey the children, but then he would renew his attention to the blocks. As he patted the blocks lovingly into place, a quiet content smile would occasionally cross his face.

Sometimes he would go to the art and paper construction table and cautiously try to invent some small telescope or binoculars out of construction paper, cardboard paper tubes, tape, and poster paint. But he always worked by himself and would shrink away into a corner of the table if other children arrived. He would leave the art table shortly thereafter, returning to his blocks.

Ming only left solitary play to join in group activities when compelled to do so, for snack time, lunchtime, music time, or story time. Both teachers had talked and worried about Ming. Is he a very shy or reserved child—*or* is he in the very early stages of learning English—*or* is he receiving cultural guidance from home? Perhaps he is dealing with a reserved temperament *and* very early English language skills *and* cultural guidance from home that he is trying to respect and adhere to?

Teacher Ranjita often got down on her knees to Ming's level, put her arm around his shoulders and spoke to him warmly, while trying to make eye contact. She talked to him about his block constructions or his latest creation at the cardboard and paper construction table. She would occasionally encourage him to speak to another child who was in the same activity area and show that child what he was creating. But Ming always shrugged off these efforts by teacher Ranjita, with an alarmed look on his face. He never made eye contact with his teacher, always casting his eyes down while she spoke to him. He pulled back from her and tried to move away.

Teacher Eduardo believed that if they simply respected Ming's preferences for solitary play and made the classroom a secure place for him he would eventually begin to make friends with both teachers and with some of the children. "Not every child has to be an extrovert," said teacher Eduardo. "The world needs introverts also. As a child, I always hated it when people tried to change me into something that I felt I just wasn't meant to be."

But teacher Ranjita responded: "I think that developmentally appropriate practice has it completely right that the most important contribution we can make to children's social and emotional competence is to establish a personal, nurturing, and responsive relationship with every child. I don't feel like I know how to do that with Ming. Since he is so solitary, I'm worried about his eventual readiness for public school kindergarten if he doesn't develop more social interaction skills" (Copple & Bredekamp, 2009). Both teachers tried to find books about "shy" children in their local libraries—or at the library in the 4-year state college where they took courses at night and on weekends. They also frequently consulted developmentally appropriate practice sources, and took heart from the emphasis on individual ways children have of showing both their emotional and social development—and how these ways might be culturally guided. They also reviewed NAEYC position statements and publications about dual language learners—and the guidance about dual language learners that their state's early childhood departments made available (NAEYC, 2009).

They knew that his grandparents did not speak English. His parents were apparently proficient enough in English that they had been able to fill out the intake form and speak briefly to the director of First Street Preschool. Then the parents had virtually disappeared into their busy lives.

Teachers Ranjita and Eduardo tried several times to reach Ming's parents in the hope that they could learn more about Ming's home life and early upbringing, but it was very hard to do so. Both teachers had families of their own, and each was also taking college courses at night, trying to ultimately complete a bachelor's degree. Their own weekends were very busy—which was also the case with Ming's parents. Ming's grandparents spoke only a few phrases of English. When either teacher tried to speak to Ming's grandparents at drop-off or pick-up time, the grandparents shook their heads with a slightly alarmed look on their faces. They seemed concerned that the teachers wanted to talk to them at all. Telephone calls home by the teachers also only resulted in strained "nonconversations" with the grandparents, since the parents were not home.

Neither teacher spoke Chinese, although Ranjita was able to borrow a Chinese language instruction tape from the college library where she took her courses. Both teachers tried to master a few phrases in Chinese, and Ming looked up with a small smile when the teachers used these phrases with him. None of the other parents spoke Chinese, and since Ming's family was the only Chinese family in the neighborhood served by the preschool, it was not possible to find a volunteer who could help with translation. Neither could this small, modestly funded preschool afford the professional translator services that could be obtained in the large city an hour and a half away.

However, there was one time in the day when Ming really brightened and lost his serious and reserved demeanor: music time. He sat up, smiled, and looked alertly at the classroom's small supply of musical instruments when they were brought out from the cupboard and discussed. If a few small musical instruments were left in the classroom, Ming could often be found playing with these by himself—although he would leave the area and return to his blocks or his paper constructions if other children tried to join in and play musical instruments with him. But clearly his favorite time of the week was Thursday afternoons when a young high school student doing community service would bring his guitar and sing children's songs. Ming seemed fascinated with the guitar and gradually learned the words to the songs, which he sang softly to himself in English.

After about eleven months at First Street Preschool, Ming attracted the friendship of 3-year-old Maria, who was also quite shy—a petite Latina with a mop of curly dark hair. Ming would let Maria sit near him as he built large constructions with the hollow blocks. Occasionally, he would talk to Maria in English, briefly explaining what he was building, and eventually, Maria, who was bilingual, would quietly pick up a block and suggest its placement. But at other times she would also leave the block building area to paint by herself on the art easel.

On the outdoor patio Ming would build high double walls of the hollow blocks in a large U-shape with a space in the middle. Once when Juan and Cole, two very active and energetic boys, tried to drive their trucks into this U-shaped construction calling it their "garage," Ming retreated entirely from his work into the shadows of the patio overhang. Silently, he watched with a fearful and concerned look as the boys demolished parts of his building.

Peering out, half-hidden by the bookcase that held the other hollow blocks, he watched anxiously until Juan and Cole became bored with the "garage" and took their trucks elsewhere. Then he quietly approached his U-shaped structure and built it carefully back up again till it almost reached the height of his shoulders. Concerned, teacher Eduardo spoke to Juan and Cole, reminding them not to break up another child's block buildings.

Teacher Eduardo also said to teacher Ranjita as she passed by, "It's almost as if Ming is building something to protect himself from the other children—a kind of double wall with space in between each wall." Teacher Ranjita nodded back. She knelt down by Ming and looked him directly in the eyes, trying again to put an arm around his shoulders. Ming shrank back slightly and averted his eyes but stood still near his teacher. Teacher Ranjita spoke briefly to Ming, asking if he would like any help in protecting his blocks.

"We have a sign here, Ming," said teacher Ranjita, showing him a stop sign encased in plastic lamination. "We can put this on your blocks as a sign to the other children that you are still working here and they should not try to knock anything over." Ming looked very briefly at teacher Ranjita and then casting his eyes down slowly shook his head to say no.

After this teacher Ranjita renewed her efforts to arrange a home visit with Ming's parents. Finally she was successful, and both teachers arrived at the family's small apartment late one Saturday afternoon. Both parents seemed very nervous. Mr. Tan, Ming's father, spoke very little and seemed fairly reserved himself. Speaking fluent English, Mrs. Tan was quite outgoing and plainly expressed her concerns that the teachers perhaps had found Ming to be poorly behaved. Several times during the teachers' explanations she asked, "But is he obedient? Is he being respectful?"

Some discussion ensued in which Mr. and Mrs. Tan expressed their feelings that Ming's shyness in school was not a problem, since he did speak out unreservedly when playing with his siblings and two cousins who frequently visited. Reassured by this, both teachers explained that, as they all wanted Ming to be successful in public kindergarten next year, it would be good for him to learn to interact more easily with both teachers and children. Both teachers also learned that Mr. and Mrs. Tan almost always spoke English with Ming and his siblings.

Teachers Ranjita and Eduardo also discovered that Mr. and Mrs. Tan had a computer at home and were both pursuing computer science degrees.

Both teachers knew that they could access the well-worn computer in the director's office to send emails—and even photos of Ming in class to his parents. The parents were delighted with this offer. Both parents also suggested that they could show Ranjita and Eduardo translation software that might be used on their smartphones, if they had access to smartphones (Nemeth & Simon, 2013).

After this home visit, Ming began to speak a few words to the teachers, especially when music was involved. One day, he briefly mentioned to teacher Eduardo that his parents had bought him a second-hand guitar for his birthday, and then he smiled. But he quickly looked down and began to move away as Eduardo warmly encouraged him to talk more about the guitar, trying to look directly into Ming's eyes and reaching out to pat his hand.

Three months later, this same withdrawn child was astonishing teachers Ranjita and Eduardo as they watched him smile and talk with student teacher Anita. Ming and the student teacher were making paper hats together. Anita rarely looked directly into Ming's eyes, but focused on the paper hat and conversed about that. "Oh my," she said, "It is hard to get this sticky tape around this corner." Ming struggled with the tape himself but managed to get off a piece and wound it around the corner of his paper hat. "Very sticky tape," he said, glancing briefly at his teacher.

Anita fleetingly returned his glance and then looked down again at their mutual play objects. "There," she said, "I'm finished. I'm going to put it on my head!" As she did so, she quickly looked at Ming and said, "I suppose I look pretty funny." He smiled briefly saying softly, "Yes, funny." then his eyes slid down again toward his own paper hat.

Naptime followed lunch, and finally the three adults were able to quietly talk together around a table in a corner of the room. The Ranjita and Eduardo said, "Anita, we want to learn from you." Anita hesitated and slowly said, "I am just a student teacher. I don't know how much you can learn from me." "We see ourselves as a community of learners here no matter how small the community is." said Ranjita firmly. "We can always learn from one another, so please tell us, Anita. Why do you think Ming is responding to you so well?"

"I don't know for sure," said Anita, "but I am thinking it may have something to do with his discovery that I play the trumpet and the saxophone. It turns out he is fascinated by these instruments. He lives near a high school and walks down with his grandparents or his parents when they are home on weekends to see the marching band practice."

"A trumpet," said Ranjita. "I knew he was interested in music, but I never thought of a trumpet. I guess, well, I wonder if I was letting a bit of stereotyping get in my way. I could tell he was interested in the guitar, but because he didn't seem to speak English and his grandparents speak only Chinese, I thought he was interested more in string instruments and perhaps ones from China." "Well," said Anita, "when I saw how much he responded to the high school student who played guitar the first week I was here, I asked him about musical instruments he might play."

Anita blushed. "I come from a very musical family. We did not have much money, but my mother and father would look for used musical instruments, and we had a neighbor who would help us repair them. We all played. It became just a family thing to do in the evenings and on weekends. It turns out that Ming's family also loves to play musical instruments."

"*How* did you find *that* out?" asked Eduardo. "We've hardly been able to get a word out of him about musical instruments."

"Well, do you remember when I brought in my own trumpet toward the end of the first week?" said Anita.

"Yes," said both Ranjita and Eduardo. "We do. But that was such a busy day for us because it was still the beginning of a semester. So I didn't notice what happened."

"Well," said Anita, "Ming came over and looked at the trumpet and fingered it and tried to play it a little although it was a little big for him. Then he told me that his mother had bought a little trumpet for the family that was just right for him, but it had already broken."

"He didn't look at me as he said this, and I didn't look at him directly in the eyes, either. I just said, 'My neighbor fixes trumpets, saxophones, and all kinds of instruments, and he is very kind. He doesn't charge money. He does it in the evening for fun.' Then, Ming said without looking up at me, 'Would he fix mine?' And I said, 'Absolutely, I am sure he would.'"

"I haven't seen any trumpet coming to class," said teacher Eduardo.

"No, he hasn't yet done that. But from time to time, he talks to me about his trumpet, and this week he looked at me in the eyes briefly as he talked about it. And I always looked back at him—just briefly—and encouraged him to bring it when he feels ready," Anita elaborated.

"Wow! But why do you look at him only briefly?" asked Eduardo.

Anita reflected for a minute and then said, "My younger sister was very shy—very, very shy—and from the time I was about eleven or twelve, I tried to figure out how to help her. We didn't have anyone around to advise us, so it was just kind of trial and error."

"I noticed that if I looked at her too long directly in her eyes, or if I put my arms around her to give her a hug, she would back off, and look downwards and just be quiet for a while. So I learned to make brief eye contact and not to touch her unless she asked me to. I would talk to her lightly about things that we are both interested in, like music and instruments that our family liked to try to play. I learned, I guess, to keep the focus on what we were interested in rather than on her or her reaction to me. And gradually by the time she was four and a half, she was able to maintain more eye contact with me and even to assert herself a little bit in the family."

"I also learned a lot from my best friend at Forest State College where I've been pursuing my degree in early childhood education. She is a first generation Chinese American and she has shared with me her belief that many Chinese and Chinese American children would not look teachers in the eye because it would not be respectful. Nor would their families all welcome a home visit from the teachers. In traditional Chinese culture, families would expect to go to the school to meet with the teacher.

"My friend Guan-yin says that we don't want to label a child as being introverted for well-behaved, highly-focused solitary behavior in the classroom."

"But," Ranjita broke in, "what will happen to this child when he goes to kindergarten where social interaction is so much a part of learning? I am worried."

"Well," said Eduardo, "I think maybe we have to talk with Ming's parents about cooperation among all of us to help Ming become both bilingual and bicultural. I mean, he will have the traditional Chinese culture that his grandparents especially are teaching him, and he will have the contemporary American culture that often forms the basis of what we do in this classroom. We have done that before, Ranjita, in talking with the Latino, East Indian, African American, and Vietnamese families we have in our program. Ming may be the only Chinese American child that we have had in our classroom thus far, but we can learn," he grinned. "Let's start with asking Anita to recommend some resources. And, perhaps her Chinese American colleague Guan-yin would recommend some good resources for articulating what we know and believe about biculturalism as well as bilingualism."

"Yes," said Anita, "I can do some of that. We did study some of Chinese culture in our multicultural course last year. But each of us has access to a public library, I think, and if I got you a syllabus would you like to see if you can get some of the books on interlibrary loan to start with?"

"That sounds like good guidance to us, Anita," said Ranjita and Eduardo. "But we have a lot of questions in our minds about how best to prepare Ming for public kindergarten. Kindergarten is just months away now."

QUESTIONS FOR DISCUSSION

1. One of the issues in this case is the question of Ming's basic temperament. Pioneering temperament researchers Stella Chess and Alexander Thomas (1996) explain: "Temperament can be equated to the term 'behavioral style.' Each refers to the *how* rather than the *what* (abilities and content) or the *why* (motivations) of behavior" (p. 33). While temperament seems to be inborn, it can be influenced by the environment. Chess and Thomas identify three temperament types in children. The "easy" child, the "slow-to-warm-up" child," and the "difficult" or "feisty and spirited" child. Using these three categories, which temperament would you say Ming has and why?

2. Professor Jerome Kagan, another highly regarded researcher about temperament, has called the "shy" child the "inhibited" child. His research shows that inhibited children are "highly reactive" to stimuli, especially new stimuli in their environments. Highly reactive children tended to be more fearful, quiet, and timid (Kagan & Snidman, 2004, pp. 6–18). In this case, does Ming display the characteristics of a "highly reactive," "inhibited" child? What incidents in the case support your opinion?

3. In their seminal book on developmentally appropriate practice, Carol Copple and Sue Bredekamp state that early childhood practitioners need to understand that sociocultural context and family circumstances influence learning, recognize children's developing competencies, and know about the variety of ways that children may demonstrate their developmental accomplishments (Copple & Bredekamp, 2009). In this case, how do Ming's teachers (including the student teacher, Anita) fulfill this part of developmentally appropriate practice? Please give specific examples. In this case, are there some ways that the teacher and the student teacher could improve their skills?

4. Cofounder of the NAEYC Asian Forum and professional development manager at the Institute for Advancing Excellence in Early Education, Sandy Baba, explains that, traditionally, Chinese children would be taught from an early age to "eat bitter"—to persevere, not show sadness, just do the work. Socializing children to "eat bitter" will help them prepare for difficulties in later life (personal communication, April 9, 2012). In this case, do you see any evidence that Ming may be taught, by his grandparents especially, to "eat bitter"?

5. Another important factor in Ming's development is his stage of acquisition of the English language. Experts refer to four stages that children typically move through when they are acquiring a second language: (1) home language use; (2) observation and listening period; (3) telegraphic and formulaic speech (e.g., use of a few words to try out the second language); (4) fluid language use (California Department of Education, 2009, pp. 45–51). In this case, at what stage is Ming's use of the English language? How do you know that? What specific example(s) from the case allow you to come to that conclusion?

6. For teachers Ranjita and Eduardo, how difficult is it to decide whether Ming's quiet, solitary play is due to a reserved or "shy" temperament; to his stage of English language acquisition; and/or to his efforts to adhere to cultural guidance he is receiving at home about proper behavior in school? Do they consider that it could be due to all three? Indicate where you see evidence of the teachers' struggles to make these decisions.

7. In most preschools there are at least several reserved or "shy" children. What kinds of issues arise for teachers in caring for and educating

children with this temperament? Increasingly, in preschools there can be many children whose home language is not English and who are in early stages of learning the English language. In this case, how do these two factors—reserved temperament and uncertainty about degree of English language acquisition—affect the behavior of the teachers regarding Ming? How much might be due to the teachers' own individual temperament and beliefs about approaches to fostering effective teacher–child interaction?

8. In this case, what are the other factors that might be contributing to Ming's reserve? For example, what role is played by the following elements:

    a. Ming's recent move to this new neighborhood where there seems to be no other Chinese families or Chinese-speaking individuals
    b. Ming's entry into First Street Preschool as a 3-year-old who is the only Chinese (or Chinese American) child in the school
    c. Cultural expectations expressed by his grandparents (or his parents) about "proper behavior" in school
    d. The initial lack of communication between preschool and home

    List any other factors that you think could be contributing to Ming's reserve.

9. In this case, teachers Ranjita and Eduardo have different approaches to trying to develop a good teacher–child relationship with Ming. Describe what you see as the difference in their two approaches.

10. In most busy preschool classrooms, teachers, no matter how skilled, might find that a child like Ming poses a lot of questions for teachers about the approaches most likely to be effective. From your perspective, what are the general teaching issues (or teacher–child interaction issues) faced by teachers Ranjita and Eduardo in their work with Ming? In your opinion, why are these issues for teachers?

11. In this case, do the teachers make the right amount of effort to reach Ming's parents? Are there other things that they might have tried? Do they approach his grandparents with cultural sensitivity? Should teachers Ranjita and Eduardo have made *more* effort to learn to speak Chinese in order to communicate more effectively with his grandparents? Should they have turned more to technology to help with communication?

12. Student teacher Anita is successful in establishing a relationship with Ming, using a number of strategies, such as the following:

    •   Building on an identified interest of this child—namely, music— to demonstrate her own genuine love for something similar—namely, music and the playing of instruments

- Focusing her attention on the objects that Ming is either discussing or constructing rather than on Ming's behavior or emotions
- Making only the briefest of eye contact

What are some of the other approaches that student teacher Anita uses to build a relationship with Ming? How do all these approaches help him move out of an inhibited state at school?

13. List what *you* would do to establish a good teacher–child relationship with a child like Ming.

14. T. Berry Brazelton and Joshua Sparrow, in their book *Touchpoints Three to Six* (2001), vividly describe the progress of a shy child, "Tim," including his experiences in a preschool classroom. An important advance that Tim (and Ming) makes is the development of a friendship with another reserved child. In your opinion, should teachers try to foster these kinds of friendships between shy children? If so, what would be the best approaches to use?

15. Professor Jeanne Tsai of Stanford University has extensively studied culture and emotion and concludes that preschool Asian American and Taiwanese children are more likely to indicate that a calm way of engaging in activity is preferable to an excited way (2007; Tsai et al., 2007). In your opinion, is a preference for calmness expressed by Ming?

RESOURCES FOR DELVING DEEPER

Best Practices in Early Care and Education Programs

Copple, C., & Bredekamp, S. (2009). *Developmentally appropriate practice in early childhood programs serving children from birth through age 8* (3rd ed.). Washington, DC: National Association for the Education of Young Children.

Galinsky, E. (2010). *Mind in the making: The seven essential life skills every child needs.* New York, NY: HarperCollins.

Gartrell, D. (2012). *Education for a civil society: How guidance teaches young children democratic life skills.* Washington, DC: National Association for the Education of Young Children.

Temperament and Its Influence on Children's Behavior and Development

Brazelton, T. B., & Sparrow, J. D. (2001). *Touchpoints three to six: your child's emotional and behavioral development.* Cambridge, MA: Perseus.

Chess, S., & Thomas, A. (1986). *Temperament in clinical practice.* New York, NY: Guildford Press.

Chess, S., & Thomas, A. (1996). *Temperament: Theory and practice.* New York, NY: Brunner / Mazel.

The Reserved, "Inhibited," or "Highly Reactive" Temperament and Its Influence on Children's Behavior and Development

Cain, S. (2012). *Quiet: The power of introverts in a world that can't stop talking.* New York, NY: Crown.

Kagan, J ., & Snidman, N. (2004). *The long shadow of temperament.* Cambridge, MA: Belknap Press of Harvard University Press.

Kagan, J., Snidman, N., Kahn, V., & Towsley, S. (2007). The preservation of two infant temperaments into adolescence. *Monographs of the Society for Research in Child Development, 72*(2).

Practical Recommendations for Helping the Reserved Child in a Classroom

Hirschland, D . (2008). Helping the shy, cautious, or withdrawn child: Getting to work when a youngster holds back from connections, play, and conversation. In *Collaborative intervention in early childhood: Consulting with parents and teachers of 3- to 7-year-olds* (pp. 131–146). New York, NY: Oxford University Press.

Preschool English Language Learners

California Department of Education. (2009). *Preschool English learners: Principles and practices to promote language, literacy, and learning—a resource guide* (2nd ed.). Sacramento: California Department of Education.

National Association for the Education of Young Children (NAEYC). (2009). *Where we stand: On responding to linguistic and cultural diversity.* [Washington, DC]: NAEYC. Retrieved from www.naeyc.org/files/naeyc/file/positions/diversity.pdf

Nemeth, K. N., & Simon, F. S. (2013). Using technology as a teaching tool for dual language learners in preschool through grade 3. *Young Children, 68*(1), 48–52.

Differences Among Euro-American, Chinese American, and Taiwanese Chinese Young Children Regarding What They Understand as "Happiness"

Tsai, J. L . (2007). Ideal affect: Cultural causes and behavioral consequences. *Perspectives on Psychological Science, 2*(3), 242–259. doi:10.1111/j.1745-6916.2007.00043.x

Tsai, J. L., Louie, J. Y., Chen, E. E., & Uchida, Y. (2007). Learning what feelings to desire: Socialization of ideal affect through children's storybooks. *Personality and Social Psychology Bulletin, 33*(1), 17–30.

Home–Preschool Relationships with Diverse Families

Halgunseth, L. C., Peterson, A., Stark, D. R., & Moodie, S. (2009). *Family engagement, diverse families, and early childhood education programs: An integrated review of the literature.* Retrieved from www.naeyc.org/files/naeyc/file/research/FamEngage.pdf

Practical Suggestions and a List of Programs That
Serve Diverse Families Well

National Association for the Education of Young Children (NAEYC). (Feb. 24, 2012). Engaging diverse families. Retrieved from www.naeyc.org/ecp/trainings/edf

Sky-High Energy in Classroom 5

with Teresa Gonczy O'Rourke and Ed Greene

It's mid-autumn at Children First Inc. Preschool, located in the working-class and middle-income suburb Francisville, a bustling Southern community with a diverse population that includes both African American and Latino neighborhoods. This full-day, full-year NAEYC-accredited preschool serves 74 children total (one class of 4-year-olds only with 18 students, two classes of combined 3- and 4-year-olds each with 16 students, and two classes of 2-year-olds each with 12 students). Mary Woods, the program's Euro-American executive director, is a soft-spoken classroom veteran with 20 years of teaching experience and a master's degree in early childhood education—as well as firm convictions about best practices in both classroom management and family engagement.

In Classroom 5, two highly active boys—Elijah and Daniel Caldwell, 4-year-old African American twins—are threatening to wreak havoc in a classroom of 3- and 4-year-olds. Even the two experienced teachers in this class of 16 children feel overwhelmed. The children race around the classroom and the outdoor play yard, teasing and shouting at one another—and erupting into aggression that threatens to become chronic conflict.

Classroom 5's lead teacher, African American Susanna York, is working toward her master's degree and has 3 years of classroom experience, but is new to Children First. Rosa Cardenas, the other teacher in Classroom 5, is also new to Children First. She is struggling to complete courses toward a bachelor's degree at Foyer College, the 4-year university that is a 45-minute commute from her home. She has an associate degree from a nearby community college.

Elijah and Daniel, the twins who are so intensely active, are also new to Children First. Their parents, Doris and George Caldwell, have a third child as well, a high-energy 2-year-old who also attends Children First. They are professionals who work downtown in urban Putnam, commuting over an hour to do so. Doris had originally trained as a teacher but then chose to enter the business world, so that both parents could save money toward the eventual college expenses of their children. She is still completing courses toward an MBA and takes some of her courses at night right after work. George, a project manager in a large local business, typically picks up the boys after school and looks after them until his wife gets home.

Teacher Rosa Cardenas is completely bilingual in both Spanish and English, and teacher Susanna York speaks some Spanish as well as fluent English.

"Expulsion may be our only option. Our classroom is absolutely over-whelmed by these twins. Mary, I'm telling you the situation has become im-possible," teacher Susanna forcefully gesticulated at the executive director of the preschool.

"We just cannot go on like this," Susanna continued. "These children tear up the classroom day after day, sometimes racing wildly through the play yard and in and out of the classroom. We can't even get them to sit long enough to focus on just about anything. They can't be safely inside the classroom at all, and circle time is just disastrous. We have to keep all the children outside for most of the time so there's enough teacher coverage for all the children. But that's not right for all the other children who could ben-efit from greater engagement with all the other activities that are best done indoors. And outside, on the twins' bad days, they're hitting other children as they race past them and just spiraling each other into extremes of silliness and giddiness and emotional intensity. It is just an utterly impossible situ-ation." Susanna's brown eyes framed by a soft Afro fixed on Mary's face.

An equally intelligent pair of blue eyes looked steadily back at Susanna from Mary's lined face, her blond hair curling softly outwards from her rosy pink skin. "Susanna, I know what you are saying. I've been director here at Children First for the last 15 years, and I have never quite seen a year like this in Classroom 5. I recognize that you have a huge challenge with Elijah and Daniel, the twins. It's really hard to cope well with their behavior, let alone care for and educate these two boys and the other fourteen."

Susanna spoke up forcefully, "Mary, it's gotten even worse in the last week. Yesterday was the very worst day that we've had. Elijah and Daniel shot back and forth across the play yard with the eggbeaters that we had put out at the water table for the children to use in their science activity. They grabbed those eggbeaters and were marching up and down the play yard, raising their arms and just shouting, 'We're going to make jello, jello, jello!'"

"They were running back and forth at first, just shouting all of this with all of the other children trying to focus in on what they were doing but being so distracted—and some of them a bit scared as well. Marching back and forth, the twins kept hoisting these eggbeaters, shouting. They weren't look-ing where they were going, and they were colliding into the other children and frightening them."

"Eventually," Susanna continued, "they landed at the water table and just whipped and whipped soapy water into so much frothiness that it foamed out all over the little patio and the other children just stepped back and stayed away from the science activity that they should have been en-joying and learning from. Then they grabbed one another and just hopped gleefully from one foot to the other circulating around the water table and continuing to scream, 'Jello, we're making jello!'—and that was just one 10-minute episode during a morning that had several episodes of unfocused intense and wild behavior. It may have been the worst 10 minutes of the morning, but there were other periods of time when they just could not sit still and their intensity led to aggression."

Elijah and Daniel were tall, wiry, 4-year-old twins, who had been at Children First since the beginning of September. Strong, active boys, they seemed always in motion. They particularly liked to play with anything that involved a ball. There was a short basketball hoop on the patio, just outside the classroom, and they obsessively shot a basketball into that hoop over and over again. They could toss a softball between the two of them for long periods of time, while staying in one place.

But sometimes they would take off unpredictably across the small play yard, tossing the ball back and forth between the two of them. It was at times like these, when they were very focused on their play with the ball, that they were most likely to hurt other children. They did not hurt the other children intentionally. They were simply totally preoccupied with their enjoyment of their play and of each other. But the other children were already beginning to decide that they did not want to play with Elijah and Daniel. And, alarmed, some children were beginning to hit back, as the twins moved in their hyperactive fashion among them. Teachers Susanna and Rosa often spoke to each other about their concerns that the hurly-burly of the twins was causing a chaotic atmosphere in the classroom.

The few times when all the children came together as a group and were expected to sit were near disasters. Neither twin could sit quietly for even a few minutes of story time. They fidgeted and squirmed, sometimes rolling around on the rug and giggling intensely. Rosa would try to sit each twin on either side of her, stroking their hair and patting their backs in a sometimes successful effort to calm them. Snack time had been particularly challenging because initially the twins had been seated at the same table. The teachers had felt that this would help the twins become acclimated to their new classroom. But the twins virtually shouted at one another as they grabbed for food. All the other children at the table shrank back, and one little girl with an especially sensitive temperament clapped her hands over her ears with a pained look on her face. The teachers quickly realized that they needed to separate the twins. But even at separate tables, Elijah and Daniel would try to gleefully call out to one another. Their active movements at times caused milk to be spilled and food to go flying off the table onto the floor. They would also grab for food, and the other children both feared and resented the twins' impulsive behavior.

"*Es muy malo*," Rosa sighed deeply, "But I think expulsion is going to have to happen, Mary." She spoke in her softly accented voice, which rose barely to a whisper, so uncertain was she about her opinion on this painful issue. "I know I haven't had as much experience as you, Susanna," she said, turning to her. "With 3 years' experience and your BA degree in early childhood education, you have a certain expertise that I have not yet acquired; I only have 1 year of teaching experience and my AA. But I *am* taking a course in mental health and early childhood at Foyer College. And in that course, I have learned that often these high energy children have undiagnosed special needs, like ADHD. Sometimes really active, intense children are on the autism spectrum. We just don't have the capacity here to work with children like that," she said wistfully.

Tall and athletic teacher Susanna turned and anxiously scrutinized the faces of both Mary and Rosa. She then arose and strode toward the window in Mary's small office, where she could see parents picking up the few remaining children on the playground at the end of the day.

With firm conviction in her voice, Mary spoke, "Of course we must be careful here. When any two African American boys like Elijah and Daniel are acting so intensely and energetically, we always want to be careful. It is so easy to experience boys like this as problems rather than try to see their strengths. These boys are creative, and their extroverted temperaments together with all this energy means they are likely to be leaders someday."

"Yes," Mary continued, "I realize that bias can always play a role in this, and I know of course that Rosa knows this too. In another program that I worked in, some of the teachers were clearly biased against African American boys and Latino boys also. When that substitute teacher came into the classroom to help us out last month, I thought she looked at Elijah and Daniel with some real bias. She saw these boys almost as personal threats rather than trying to understand them as boys who had great strengths as well."

"Yes," said Susanna, turning back to Mary, "Rosa and I had to talk to her very candidly about implicit bias. She didn't feel like she was prejudiced at all, and probably she wasn't in the overt way that we all recognize. But it is so easy for implicit bias to creep into our assessments of African American and Latino boys—and I suppose girls as well. But I think boys have a much harder time. They just seem to threaten us female teachers more."

"Well, Susanna," said Mary, with a slight smile, "does recognizing this bias change your mind at all? A few minutes ago you were close to advocating expulsion, remember?"

"No," said Susanna slowly, with a look of sadness crossing her face. She spoke rather quietly for such a strong woman. "I hate to even think about this, Mary," she said, her eyes casting downward. "I just hate it. I know what expulsion will mean for these boys. It will mean that they think they are not good enough to belong at Children First Preschool. And that's just horrible. It's hard enough for African American boys to develop a strong, positive sense of self, since so many of the messages coming from the public are so negative about our community's boys. And I am concerned that feeling of not being good enough is likely to go with them into their next school—if they can even find a school that will accept them. But we have to think about the other children as well. They deserve our attention and time too—and they are not getting it."

"First of all, I will rearrange my schedule here in the office and plan to come into your classroom over the next few days," said Mary. "I'll be able to see more clearly many of the good ideas that I'm sure you are using already. I also have some ideas for classroom and family engagement strategies that might help. We've had other children like this over the years, and there are definitely approaches that we can take that will help Elijah and Daniel. Let's see if we can get a substitute teacher in during naptime tomorrow and then we can talk about it together."

"What kinds of ideas?" asked Susanna skeptically. "Can you give us just a quick general idea? I've also had some experience with children like this in the past, but never with two of them at one time, in one classroom. The only thing I can think of is medication."

"There's not enough time tonight to discuss this, as I know that I have an appointment in a half hour across town, and Rosa has to get to her evening class at Foyer College," said Mary. "But in general, there are classroom strategies and family engagement strategies that I have seen that are successful and match what research-based best practices tell us are likely to work. So I feel confident that they may work well in this case. Let me spend the time that I have left here tonight now trying to get a substitute teacher for tomorrow's naptime."

All three women gathered their belongings and prepared to leave the school as nighttime was falling, Susanna and Rosa with heavy hearts and Mary with some hopefulness.

The next day, both teachers entered Mary Woods' office at naptime. On the table were several large bowls, food coloring, construction paper, scissors, tape, glitter glue, and strips of brightly colored ribbon. Also, two large cardboard cartons were stacked in the corner. Both teachers glanced at the art materials and looked quizzically at Mary. "We'll get to this in just a moment," said Mary. "The first thing I want to say to you both is that you have made very strong efforts to work with these children. There's always more for all of us to learn. But I hope that you feel proud of yourselves for all that you have tried to do so far this year."

"Thanks, Mary. It's been a rough morning, as you know, since you came to help us in the classroom. So your words are much appreciated," sighed Susanna. Mary could see both teachers visibly relax as she went on to praise their specific actions.

Mary's time in Classroom 5 had allowed her to observe once again the strong degree of classroom organization. Musical instruments, as well as brightly colored construction paper, colored pencils, markers, scissors, and pens were among the materials that were well-stored on open-ended shelves.

She had recently reread an excellent resource, a book called *Challenging Behavior in Young Children* by Barbara Kaiser and Judy Sklar Rasminsky (2017). She had noticed that the authors called for materials that are easy for small, busy hands to handle since children with challenging behaviors often lack fine motor skills. The authors had suggested having large brushes, toothbrushes, cotton balls, wallpaper scraps, fabric, feathers, and magazine photos available in order to make art projects more attractive for children who find it difficult to sit still and use their fine motor skills. Mary knew that the twins could be drawn into projects that responded to their strong interest in ball games and similar activities.

This focus on creating projects that reflected this interest that so engaged them would help them develop greater executive function skills as they planned out their projects. She hoped that the teachers could build on these activities to develop some project that would focus on problems or questions that the children would study together with the teachers.

"We'll discuss some classroom strategies in a few minutes," said Mary, "but I deeply believe that we must engage families first when situations like this arise. And we need to engage them around some positives that we see in their children. And we should make sure we see the strengths in these parents first. The Caldwells are exceptionally devoted to their children. They are willing to work long hours trying to make sure that there will be plenty of savings to send their children to college. But they are difficult to engage, I know," Mary continued. "The Caldwells are so busy. There were some problems with the boys in their previous preschool, something that I knew existed, but they are really reluctant to talk about. So their anxiety will be sparked by any concerns that we express."

"I completely agree with your assessment," nodded Susanna, while Rosa smiled also. "I think the Caldwells are somewhat burned out with their three active children since their 2-year-old is also very energetic. Fortunately, they both seem to have a lot of energy as well, but still it's got to be hard."

"Well, we've already had one parent conference with them, at the very beginning of the school year. And we were able to express many positive things about the children to each of them," said Susanna, leaning forward her chair, her brown eyes brightening. "So I think that there's some level of trust that's already been built up. Given that the Caldwells have had trouble with other preschools, we've been very careful to stress mainly positive aspects of their children's experience here."

"We need to think through very carefully how we're going to bring up our concerns to the Caldwells," replied Mary with a worried look on her face. "This is very delicate especially because I think that we may ultimately end up needing to recommend a comprehensive evaluation for each of the children. Parents can feel so threatened and defensive when this occurs—and sometimes the more devoted the parent, the more likely this is going to occur."

"Why don't we see what we can accomplish with some different class-room strategies? Perhaps we can persuade these children to calm down a bit, and if that happens, then we'll be able to report some progress to the parents. Why don't we discuss what you've already tried?" Mary inquired.

Teachers Susanna and Rosa spent the next 15 minutes describing some of the strategies they had already used in the classroom and in the play yard. They ticked them off one by one:

- Providing multiples of balls and purchasing two plastic basketball hoops so that there would always be sufficient toys for each twin— as well as the other children, when they were all outside or inside together
- Assigning one teacher to shadow the two children as much as possible while also trying to keep an eye on a few other children
- Creating a visual calendar of the day so that all the children could anticipate exactly what was going to happen and when
- Inviting all the children to participate in drafting the classroom rules and in encouraging the others to adhere to them
- Setting forth clear expectations at the beginning of each activity for how the children should behave during the activity and explaining why this is necessary
- Encouraging the children to develop stories about objects they made or liked to play with so that they could stand and tell these stories during circle time, when it was their turn, rather than sitting the entire time

Mary listened carefully to her teachers, and after they had finished, she praised each specific teacher behavior. Going over her notes from the conversation with them, she pointed out all of the positive actions that the teachers were taking and why this kind of planning and focused presentations by the children mattered so much to the development of self-regulation.

Turning toward the materials, Mary then lifted the supplies and placed them in front of the teachers. "Mary, we already use some of these materials in our classroom," protested Rosa, raising her hand up toward her face and shrugging her shoulders. "So I'm not sure what they're doing here now."

Smiling, Mary said, "These were just a few pieces of found art. You'll be able to find more in the yard if you look carefully. There's also a teachers' resource center in the city where I live. Since it's an hour away from here, I don't anticipate that you'll be going to it, but I can bring you some materials. The key takeaway here as we look at these materials is not *whether* the children work with them in the classroom but *when* they work with them."

Mary continued, "Both of you know that the research shows that self-regulation and executive function are comprised of three components: inhibitory control (resisting habits, temptations, or distractions); working memory (mentally holding and using information); and cognitive flexibility (adjusting to change) [Diamond, Barnett, Thomas, & Munro, 2007].

"I'm suggesting that the children begin each morning as they come in by sitting down at a table and focusing their minds on designing something or working on a project that interests them deeply."

"They usually rush into the yard. I'm not sure we'll be able to get them to stop," said Susanna, combing her fingers through her hair, a gesture that she typically did when she was feeling uncertain about something.

"*Si, imposible*," said Rosa softly, shaking her head firmly from side to side and staring at Mary skeptically.

As she listened to the teachers, Mary reflected that as soon as the teachers were ready, she wanted to help them learn about developing play plans with the children, visual or combined visual and written plans describing in what activity center they will play and what they will do. She had learned about play plans in a workshop on the Tools of the Mind curriculum (Bodrova & Leong, 2007). She knew that it would be important for the teachers to allocate plenty of time for play, especially dramatic play in which the children could act out different roles using props and toys. Since the twins were so interested in making imaginary jello, Mary thought that a jello-themed activity could be extended.

"Well, let's see what we can do to make it somewhat irresistible to them," said Mary, bringing out a series of boxes of different colored jello in large graduated bowls, food coloring, plastic dish bins, whisks, measuring cups, measuring spoons, pipettes, large turkey basters and small bottles of dish soap. Mary explained, "We know that developmentally appropriate practice [Copple & Bredekamp, 2009] tells us that children learn best when learning experiences are active, meaningful, and connected. And I've brought you also my copy of Marilou Hyson's [2008] book on enthusiastic and engaged learners. She gives lots of good ideas about developing activities from children's own interests.

"These children are expressing an interest in jello," she affirmed, "so best to build on that interest with two types of projects. One would be a combined science, math, and art project where the children could work with one teacher to develop and use a 'jello factory.'"

Smiling, Mary said, "Let's start with the phrase, 'I wonder,' because young children are always wondering. 'I wonder' what would happen if we tried to make a jello factory? What would happen if we put tiny drops of food coloring into our measuring cups with water? How tiny can we make them? What happens if we mix the red color with blue? With yellow? How many different colors of imaginary jello can we make?" Mary brought out the markers and the construction paper and said, "We can ask Elijah and Daniel, 'Let's see if we can make a sign for our jello factory. We can write down all the flavors our factory can make and see if Juan and Ella and Ruby could tell us which flavors are their favorites. We can take our clipboards and go to each child in the classroom and ask them to tell us which flavors they like best.' Then we can count with them and see if we can help the children figure out which flavors are the most popular. We can even cut out squares of construction paper and help them make a graph of the different flavors and their respective votes."

Mary smiled, "It won't be easy at first to persuade them to inhibit and regulate their movements in order to engage with these tasks, but if we keep trying, we'll capture their interest and their motivation to channel their energies into learning."

Mary went on to describe another project, one that would involve building on the twins' interest in games with balls, including lightweight whiffle balls and plastic bats. She said, "Let's also initiate this project by using the phrase, 'I wonder.' Let's wonder if a baseball stadium might be built. We could encourage the boys to build a baseball stadium with unit blocks. We could make admission tickets and signs out of paper; food that could be sold and eaten; menus and simple recipes for the food. We could obtain books about baseball or work with the children to make their own books. All these activities involve reflection, planning, focus, inhibition of unfocused movement, the development and use of working memory for all the details related to the project and the practice of the mental flexibility needed to switch back and forth between tasks."

As Mary spoke, ticking off some details, she thought, "This will definitely help. It's building the neuronal connections in the reasoning part of the brain and then the connections between the reasoning part and the emotion-centered part." She relayed her thoughts to both teachers and was relieved to see that they were listening and engaging with these ideas.

"I am concerned, Mary, that this might not work at all," protested Susanna, her voice rising as she straightened in her chair. "Can just a few minutes of planning and reflection really help? They'll leave that behind in just a few minutes and go back to their wild behavior!"

"It may only be a few minutes at first, Susanna," said Mary firmly, "But we can add on activities like this, so that a few minutes starts to grow into more minutes and then ultimately into perhaps 5 to 10 minutes of sitting and focusing in an intentional way. Ultimately, this will help them develop what you know is called *executive function*: the ability to plan, to channel attention, remember things, and follow through. I've seen this happen with other children. It's not the only thing that we'll try, of course. It's just that this is something that we would start off the day with. Ultimately, they can be helped to develop a written or visual plan—a play plan—for how they would play in the jello factory area."

Susanna stood up and paced the room. "This is good, but we need more than this. A friend of mine who is a teacher at another NAEYC-accredited preschool in our community told me about a mental health consultant that they used when they had some children with challenging behaviors in their classroom. She said that this mental health consultation service was funded by a local foundation and that the consultant came once a week—more often in the beginning—and was really helpful. I'm not sure that this will be enough to change my mind about expulsion being necessary. But I'm willing to try."

"Great, Susanna!" smiled Mary, "I'm aware of the mental health agency, and I was going to suggest it, but I'm so glad that you came up with the idea first. I know both you and Rosa share my conviction that we don't want to see these boys be expelled if we can possibly avoid it. This is one of the things I admire about the both of you."

"In the meantime, we can try out some other ideas that have worked well in the past with other children with challenging behaviors," continued Mary. "For example, let's tape off a spot on the grass for the children to practice controlled movements—even pretend fighting. Let's try some yoga after the children come in from free play outside. With enough calming music, these focused actions and the deep breathing that are part of yoga practice with children may also help them develop executive function. We can also make sure that we assign Elijah and Daniel some special jobs that they can each carry out in the classroom. Sometimes, giving children these kinds of responsibilities will help."

"*Bueno, mis amigas,*" said Rosa, with a happy look in her face. "Since I'm in charge of snack and lunch time, I had already decided that we would give each of these children responsibility for helping me wash and set the tables and for fetching the food from the kitchen and then for cleaning up with me afterwards. In the course that I'm taking, my professor talks a lot about giving each child specific positive praise for small actions that are positive. I think I can do this with each child if Susanna can briefly keep the others out in the play yard while we are setting up the tables. I could also try to do this after the children are finished with their meals, while the other 14 are divided into small groups to go into the bathroom under Susanna's supervision."

"If it's too challenging initially to persuade both boys to carry out their jobs, just let me know, and I'll come to the classroom right after the snacks and lunch and help you get these routines established," reassured Mary with a warm smile. "Once they know what to do and we've given the specific positive praise that reinforces the mindset that they can grow the capacity to take on responsibility and resist the impulse just to jump up from the table, I feel sure they'll gradually develop the habit and will feel good about themselves as helpers in the classroom," said Mary. As she looked at the concerned faces of the two women in front of her, Mary reflected that they were accepting her suggestions despite their initial misgivings. She thought back to other occasions when teachers have not been able to shake the impulse themselves to focus primarily on telling children what they were doing wrong, rather than what they are doing right. The teachers' focus on what they did not like about children's behavior only reinforced the conviction that somehow they were "bad children."

"Well, I want our meetings to be problem-solving sessions in which we give each other specific positive praise also," added Mary, "Let's not save it completely for communication with the children—although that really matters of course. But each of you needs this kind of reinforcement also. What you're doing is not easy, and I want this to be a safe space for exchanging ideas and feeling accepted for our efforts.

"I can't guarantee that this problem will be completely solved," Mary continued, "but I can assure you that you will have my utmost respect for trying to solve it. I will do my best to make sure that we keep reaching out to others for new ideas, including ideas from the mental health consultant, whom we should definitely try to bring on board."

"Is it possible for you to spend even more time in our classroom, Mary?" inquired Susanna. "I know that any indoor activity is especially challenging. These two children take up so much attention that Rosa and I feel like we have to split up often. One of us tries to shadow them, since they tend to stick together so much—and that means one of us is trying to give the other 14 children what they need. An extra pair of hands in the classroom would be really welcome."

"*Si, estaba bien,*" sighed Rosa. "I go home each night so exhausted. And I still need to study when I get home. So your help would be really welcome."

"Yes, I've been thinking about that also," said Mary. "I'll rearrange my schedule for the next 2 weeks and come into your classroom for an hour each day." But Mary reflected that she would not be able to keep up this arrangement for long. She was already working 12-hour days. She could try to work additional hours from home at night on the computer to complete some of the tasks that she would ordinarily be doing during the day. But she couldn't do that for longer than 2 weeks without shortchanging the time she need for sleep, exercise, and preparation of healthy meals—all necessary for her own long-term health. Mary decided that she could use this hour in their classroom to model teaching strategies and to give the teachers time to try out new techniques with a smaller group of children—and then resume her more normal schedule.

"We also have to get the parents engaged in problem solving around this," said Susanna. Mary acknowledged Susanna's point: "I know this is going to be especially challenging," she said with an anxious look on her face. "The Caldwells are now so worried about something being wrong with their boys that it's almost impossible to talk to them."

Susanna shifted uneasily in her chair, "Yes, I know that the parents take turns dropping off Elijah and Daniel in the morning, and they often don't even make eye contact with me. They just bring the boys into the classroom and turn around and leave as rapidly as possible. I can tell that they're concerned that I'm going to have some bad news for them. And there are always too many people around when George Caldwell picks up the boys at the end of the school day for me to be able to say anything to him. Not that he waits for any kind of conversation at that point either. He seems to want to collect the boys and their things and move as quickly as possible out of the classroom."

"But," she went on, "we're going to have to find a way to engage them—both parents—if we're going to be able to help Elijah and Daniel. But I simply don't have any ideas, Mary and Rosa," said Susanna, resting her head in her hands discontentedly.

"I think that they need some more instances where they're being told positive things about their children—and some specific plan—before we can bring up our concerns. They need to feel that we're fully on the side of these boys," asserted Rosa. "Otherwise, we're just going to have constant negative communication with the Caldwells, who will be alarmed and will likely become very defensive, just digging in and denying there's a problem."

"I know, I know. I know that you're right. But we just have to make sure that we're also honest with them," blurted out Susanna. "We don't know for sure yet if we can actually keep these boys here. Expulsion may be ultimately necessary if we can't work things out so that the other children are getting what they need. We cannot deprive all the other children. It's not fair to them or to their parents." Susanna leaned forward, her elbows on her knees, her head in her hands. "At some point, the parents deserve to know that we're even talking about the possibility of expulsion. And as an African American teacher myself, this is the last thing I want to find myself saying to African American parents."

"Let's just recognize, all three of us, that this is a very hard place for us to be," replied Mary, leaning across her desk and offering her hand to both teachers. "None of us have asked for this situation—neither the parents nor us."

"Well, Mary, what are we going to do about the parents?" asked Susanna, taking Mary's offered hand.

"Let's start with something a little less threatening, which is that we want to recommend that both boys have a comprehensive, in-depth assessment of both their strengths and their limitations. That's going to be threatening enough, I know," said Mary, looking directly into the eyes of each teacher in turn.

"Yes, it will be," stated Susanna firmly. "As African American parents, they'll know how many other African American children have been wrongly classified as 'special needs children'—children who must be placed in classrooms intended only for special education. They may object to any kind of evaluation of these boys. Doris Caldwell initially trained as a teacher, you know. So she's bound to know plenty about how these assessments can end up in labeling children in ways that are just plain wrong."

"I don't want to keep bringing up my course in early childhood mental health all the time," stated Rosa, "But my instructor says that she found that careful, in-depth assessment of children can result in some quite useful information. Mary, is there any agency in our community that carries out really good evaluations of children? Since I am new to this community, I don't know of any."

"The Children's Health Trust conducts excellent assessments of children," said Mary Woods, standing up and stretching her arms to the back of her head. "We have sent other children to them in the past. They're very careful. They assess children with a multidisciplinary team approach with multiple different tests. The team includes a psychiatrist, a psychologist, an occupational therapist, and a social worker. The team meets several times to look at the results of the tests and discuss them."

"Okay, this sounds better than I thought, but why a psychiatrist?" questioned Susanna. "At this agency, are they the type of professionals who put children on medication a lot? I'm *really* opposed to that," she said forcefully. "I think that young children's bodies are still growing and should not be subjected to the kinds of medications that are safer for adults to take. Mary, look, let's be honest. Does this agency typically jump to conclusions about medication?"

"No, even if they do diagnose the children with ADHD, they know a lot about safe medications and about alternative routes to managing it," replied Mary reassuringly. "For example, last year we had a child who was diagnosed by the agency team with ADHD, and they recommended neurofeedback—a way of teaching children with ADHD to change their brain waves using biofeedback. Neurofeedback—sometimes called EEG training—teaches patients to use biofeedback to consciously change their brain waves to a slower speed, which can really help children with ADHD. The Children's Health Trust biofeedback expert told me that it doesn't always work, but, it did in the case of the child from our program. Sometimes they recommend minimal amounts of medication to supplement the brain wave biofeedback, but only if it's absolutely necessary."

"I hope that we can have an honest but not too anxious conversation with the Caldwells about this," said Susanna doubtfully. "I'm not sure that we can, but I'm willing to try."

"Since you're the ones who see them everyday and need to have a continuing relationship with them, we want to have most of the communication happening between you and them." said Mary, smiling warmly at both teachers, "But let's see if I can take the lead on bringing them into my office. Then I can float the idea, and together we hopefully can gradually bring them around to agreeing to have the boys evaluated. Meantime, you can continue to find something positive about the boys' behavior every day to communicate to the Caldwells. Even if you can't communicate it to them in conversation at the end of the school day, you could send them an email, even with a photo or two of something that the boys have been doing. This will continue to build their conviction that you really care about and love their boys."

Eight weeks later they reconvened. Mary had been sent the results of the comprehensive evaluation. She wanted to go over it with both teachers before sitting down with Doris and George Caldwell. She knew that the parents would have already received their own copy, but she wanted to review it with them together with both teachers and create a plan of action for the boys at school. In the last month, the psychologist on the evaluation team had come to the school twice in order to observe the boys. The teachers looked exhausted, but eager. It had not been an easy 2 months. The new classroom strategies and the focus on solidifying a positive working relationship with the Caldwells had definitely helped. But there were still long, exhausting days in which the boys' behavior challenged every teaching skill—and every last bit of their patience.

"What did they say, Mary?" Susanna inquired anxiously Mary spoke decisively. "The Children's Health Trust team concludes that both Elijah and Daniel are exceptionally gifted. In addition to very high cognitive ability, their exceptionally intense temperaments fit the profile of many gifted children. They also feel certain that the twins have ADHD. They've been very careful about coming to this conclusion. They are recommending brainwave biofeedback as soon as possible, and believe that this will help a good deal. If it's not enough, however, they do feel that the boys can safely be given very small amounts of medication to supplement everything else that we're trying."

"Wow!" said Susanna, leaning forward in her chair, heir eyes brightening. "Exceptionally gifted! And to think we might have expelled boys who could become top leaders in our society."

"Susanna, Mary," said Rosa, "we need to realize that together we have made considerable progress on putting into place some good classroom and family engagement strategies that are starting to work. But the twins' activity level is still so high that just yesterday we discussed the possibility of having to ask the parents to work with us to find another program for them. We still haven't resolved this dilemma. And if The Children's Health Trust recommendations don't work," said Rosa, her face deeply creased with fatigue and worry, "we still might have to insist that the boys leave our school."

Both women nodded sympathetically. "Rosa, we are both trying really hard," said Susanna. "I think we are doing our utmost. Let's just hope now that the addition of brainwave biofeedback, some medication, and regular mental health consultation to us will dramatically improve the situation. But I recognize that we are still dealing with this dilemma of how to help these twins, while making sure that the other children get what they need."

QUESTIONS FOR DISCUSSION

1. In this case, what do you feel are the primary issues for the teachers? For the director? For the families? For the children?

2. In this case, the teachers are so frustrated that they recommend expulsion of the twins to their director. Walter Gilliam of Yale University (Gilliam & Shahar, 2006) found that expulsion in preschool occurs at three times the rate as in elementary school, but that these high rates of expulsion could be reduced by specific actions that support teachers better. What would you say are some of the actions that are recommended in this case that would help both teachers Susanna and Rosa? List those actions that are recommended by the director, as well as those that are developed by the teachers and discussed with the director.

3. In this case, do you think that the teachers' feelings that expulsion may be the only option are justified? How does the director respond to the teachers' frustrations? Do you agree with her response? Why or why not?

4. In this case, teacher Susanna especially voices her concern that expulsion of the twins could have a highly negative impact on the boys' sense of self and on the family in general. Do you think the teachers in this case have an obligation to balance the likely expulsion-related negative impact on a few children with their obligations to the other children in the classroom? To the families of the other children? In this case, how do they try to do this?

5. Executive function and self-regulation skills are defined by the Center on the Developing Child at Harvard University (2015) as "the mental processes that enable us to plan, focus attention, remember instructions, and juggle multiple tasks successfully" (para. 1). In this case, do you think that Elijah and Daniel have well-developed executive function and self-regulation skills? Use examples to describe why or why not.

6. The Center on the Developing Child at Harvard University (2015) goes on to further describe executive function and self-regulation skills as similar to "an air traffic control system at a busy airport [that] safely manages the arrivals and departures of many aircraft on multiple runways" (para. 1). The Center asserts that "the brain needs this skill set to filter distractions, prioritize tasks, set and achieve goals, and control impulses" (para. 1). In this case, how do the teachers help the children develop better executive function and self-regulation skills?

7. Elena Bodrova and Deborah Leong (2007) developed Tools of the Mind, an early childhood curriculum that scaffolds children's learning of self-regulation and executive functioning. One of their tools is *play planning*, where children plan orally and then use paper to represent

what they intend to do during their make-believe play In this case, do the teachers or the director talk about any general planning techniques they are using with Elijah and Daniel? How could they have done more play planning with the boys, as well as all the children in their classroom? Have you ever done play planning with children you've worked with? How did it go?

8. In their book *Challenging Behavior in Young Children*, Barbara Kaiser and Judy Sklar Rasminsky (2017) talk about needing a three-step process of understanding, preventing, and responding effectively. Describe how the teachers in this case tried to understand the boys' challenging behavior. What techniques did they use to try to prevent the behavior, such as routines, environmental cues, and so on? In your own classroom or other work with children, how have you attempted to understand children's challenging behavior? What have you done to try to preemptively prevent challenging behavior?

9. In this case, how did the teachers respond when there was challenging behavior, and do you think their responses were effective? In your experience, what have you done to respond to children's challenging behavior, and do you think it was effective?

10. In her book *Enthusiastic and Engaged Learners*, Marilou Hyson (2008) proposes that enthusiasm and engagement are the two primary dimensions of positive approaches to learning. She further describes enthusiasm as having three components— interest, pleasure, and motivation to learn—and engagement as having four components—attention, persistence, flexibility, and self-regulation. In this case, do you see any examples of teachers tapping into and encouraging these components?

11. Teacher Rosa brings up the issue of possibly undiagnosed special needs. In this case, how is the issue of diagnosis of special needs handled? Do you agree with the approaches used? Why or why not?

12. In this case, director Mary Woods emphasizes the importance of seeing the strengths in the parents of Elijah and Daniel. In your experience, what are some of the challenges involved in communicating with parents of children with challenging behaviors? How difficult is it to see strengths in the parents and the children? What have you tried or would plan to try when communicating with parents?

13. In this case, what are some of the family engagement strategies discussed? Do the teachers and the director do enough to build the potential for a strong, positive dialogue and sense of trust? What would you add and why? Are there any strategies that you disagree with? Why?

14. *Implicit bias* has been well studied by Walter Gilliam and his team (2016), who explain that it refers to the stereotypes that, in automatic and unconscious ways, drive people to make certain kinds of decisions

and to behave in certain ways. What is your own understanding of implicit bias? Have you seen or experienced implicit bias in your own personal or professional life? How does it drive teachers to stereotype children, especially boys of color? How do you think this could be prevented?

15. The Children's Health Trust, after an in-depth assessment, concludes that Elijah and Daniel are highly gifted, combining both exceptional cognitive abilities with intense temperaments. In their book, *Living with Intensity*, Susan Daniels and Michael Piechowski (2009) describe *overexcitability* as "an innate tendency to respond in an intensified manner to various forms of stimuli, both external and internal" (p. 8). How do the twins show evidence of being overexcitable?

RESOURCES FOR DELVING DEEPER

Self-Regulation and Executive Function

Bodrova, E., & Leong, D. (2007). *Tools of the mind: The Vygotskian approach to early childhood education* (2nd ed.). Upper Saddle River, NJ: Pearson/Merrill Prentice Hall.

Center on the Developing Child at Harvard University. (2015). Executive function & self-regulation. Retrieved from developingchild.harvard.edu/science/key-concepts/executive-function/

Daniels, S., & Piechowski, M. M. (2009). *Living with intensity: Emotional development of gifted children, adolescents, and adults.* Scottsdale, AZ: Great Potential Press.

Diamond, A., Barnett , W. S., Thomas, J., & Munro, S. (2007). Preschool program improves cognitive control. *Science, 318*(5855), 1387–1388. doi:10.1126/science.1151148

Posner, M. I., Rothbart, M. K., Sheese, B. E., & Voelker, P. (2014). Developing attention: Behavioral and brain mechanisms. *Advances in Neuroscience, 2014,* Article ID 405094. doi:10.1155/2014/405094

Rothbart, M. K., Sheese, B. E., & Posner, M. I. (2007). Executive attention and effortful control: Linking temperament, brain networks, and genes. *Child Development Perspectives, 1*(1), 2–7. doi:10.1111/j.1750-8606.2007.00002.x

Willingham, D. T. (2011). Ask the cognitive scientist: Can teachers increase students' self-control? *American Educator, 35*(2), 22–27.

Development of Boys of Color

Barbarin, O. A., & Crawford, G. M. (2006). Acknowledging and reducing stigmatization of African American boys. *Young Children, 61*(6), 79–86.

Barbarin, O. A., Murry, V. M., Tolan, P., & Graham, S. (2016). Development of boys and young men of color: Implications of developmental science for My Brother's Keeper Initiative. *Social Policy Report, 29*(3), 1–31.

My Brother's Keeper Initiative. (2016). Retrieved from obamawhitehouse.archives. gov/node/279811

Value of Positive Classroom Strategies to Foster Development

Copple, C., & Bredekamp, S. (2009). *Developmentally appropriate practice in early childhood programs serving children from birth through age 8* (3rd ed.). Washington, DC: National Association for the Education of Young Children.

National Association for the Education of Young Children. (n.d.). Developmentally appropriate practice (DAP). Retrieved from www.naeyc.org/DAP

Epstein, A. S. (2014). *The intentional teacher: Choosing the best strategies for young children's learning* (Rev. ed.). Washington, DC: National Association for the Education of Young Children.

Hyson, M. (2008). *Enthusiastic and engaged learners: Approaches to learning in the early childhood classroom.* New York, NY & Washington, DC: Teachers College Press and National Association for the Education of Young Children.

Kaiser, B., & Rasminsky, J. S. (2017). *Challenging behavior in young children: Understanding, preventing, and responding effectively* (4th ed.). Boston, MA: Pearson.

Mental Health Consultation

Donahue, P. J., Falk, B., & Provet, A. G. (2000). *Mental health consultation in early childhood.* Baltimore, MD: Paul H. Brookes.

Elliott, G. R., & Kelly, K. (2006). *Medicating young minds: How to know if psychiatric drugs will help or hurt your child.* New York, NY: Stewart, Tabori, & Chang.

Johnston, K., & Brinamen, C. (2006). *Mental health consultation in child care: Transforming relationships among directors, staff, and families.* Washington, DC: Zero to Three Press.

ADHD

Bloom, P. J. (2003). *Leadership in action: How effective directors get things done.* Lake Forest, IL: New Horizons.

National Technical Assistance Center for Children's Mental Health. (n.d.). {Website]. Retrieved from gucchdtacenter.georgetown.edu/

Zinsser, K. M., Denham, S. A., Curby, T. W., & Chazan-Cohen, R. (2016). Early childhood directors as socializers of emotional climate. *Learning Environments Research, 19*(2), 267–290. doi:10.1007/s10984-016-9208-7.

Family Engagement

Brazelton Touchpoints Center. (n.d.). [Website]. Retrieved from www.brazelton-touchpoints.org/

U.S. Department of Health and Human Services, Administration for Children and Families. (2016). PFCE (Parent, Family, and Community Engagement)

interactive framework. Retrieved from eclkc.ohs.acf.hhs.gov/hslc/tta-system/
family/framework

Designing Classroom Supports and Early Intervention Strategies in Promoting Social and Emotional Development

Center on the Social and Emotional Foundations for Early Learning. (n.d.). Center
on the Social and Emotional Foundations for Early Learning. Retrieved from
csefel.vanderbilt.edu

Fox, L., Dunlap, G., Hemmeter, M. L., Joseph, G. E., & Strain, P. S. (2003). *The
teaching pyramid: A model for supporting social competence and preventing
challenging behavior in young children*. Handout 4.7: Leadership Strategies.
[Nashville, TN]: Vanderbilt University, Center on the Social and Emotional
Foundations for Early Learning. Available at csefel.vanderbilt.edu/resources/
inftodd/mod4/4.7.pdf

Expulsion of Preschool Children

Gilliam, W. S., & Shahar, G. (2006). Preschool and child care expulsion and suspension: Rates and predictors in one state. *Infants & Young Children, 19*(3),
228–245. doi:10.1097/00001163-200607000-00007

Jones, D., & Levin, D. (2016, February 23). Here's why preschool suspensions are
harmful. *Education Week, 35*(22), 25. Retrieved from www.edweek.org/ew/ar-
ticles/2016/02/24/heres-why-preschool-suspensions-are-harmful.html

Turner, Cory. (2016, September 28). Bias isn't just a police problem, it's a preschool
problem. Retrieved from www.npr.org/sections/ed/2016/09/28/495488716/bi-
as-isnt-just-a-police-problem-its-a-preschool-problem

United States Department of Health and Human Services, Administration for Children and Families. (2016). *State and local action to prevent expulsion and
suspension in early learning settings*. Retrieved from www.acf.hhs.gov/sites/
default/files/ecd/state_and_local_profiles_expulsion.pdf

Implicit Bias

Cohen, G. L., Steele, C. M., & Ross, L. D. (1999). The mentor's dilemma: Providing critical feedback across the racial divide. *Personality and Social Psychology
Bulletin, 25*(10), 1302-1318.

Gilliam, W. S., Maupin, A. N., Reyes, C. R., Accavitti, M., & Shic, F. (2016). *Do early
educators' implicit biases regarding sex and race relate to behavior expectations
and recommendations of preschool expulsions and suspensions?* New Haven,
CT: Yale University Child Study Center. Retrieved from ziglercenter.yale.edu/
publications/Preschool Implicit Bias Policy Brief_final_9_26_276766_5379.pdf

Building Emotional Intelligence Skills That Help Children Regulate Their Behaviors

Bailey, C. S., Zinsser, K. M., Curby, T. W., Denham, S. A., & Bassett, H. H.
(2013). Consistently emotionally supportive preschool teachers and children's

social–emotional learning in the classroom: Implications for center directors and teachers. *Dialog, 16*(2), 131–137.

Brackett, M. A., & Rivers, S. E. (2014). Transforming students' lives with social and emotional learning. In R. Pekrun & L. Linnenbrink-Garcia (Eds.), *International Handbook of Emotions in Education* (pp. 368–388). New York, NY: Taylor & Francis.

Brackett, M. A., Rivers, S. E., & Salovey, P. (2011). Emotional intelligence: Implications for personal, social, academic, and workplace success. *Social and Personality Psychology Compass, 5*(1), 88–103. doi:10.1111/j.1751-9004.2010.00334.x

Denham, S. A., Bassett, H. H., Way, E., Kalb, S., Warren-Khot, H., & Zinsser, K. (2014). "How would you feel? What would you do?" Development and underpinnings of preschoolers' social information processing. *Journal of Research in Childhood Education, 28*(2), 182–202. doi:10.1080/02568543.2014.883558

Eggum, N. D., Eisenberg, N., Kao, K., Spinrad, T. L., Bolnick, R., Hofer, C., . . . Fabricius, W. V. (2011). Emotion understanding, theory of mind, and prosocial orientation: Relations over time in early childhood. *Journal of Positive Psychology, 6*(1), 4–16. doi:10.1080/17439760.2010.536776

Hagelskamp, C., Brackett, M. A., Rivers, S. E., & Salovey, P. (2013). Improving classroom quality with the RULER approach to social and emotional learning: Proximal and distal outcomes. *American Journal of Community Psychology, 51*(3–4), 530–543. doi:10.1007/s10464-013-9570-x

Jennings, P. A., & Greenberg, M. T. (2009). The prosocial classroom: Teacher social and emotional competence in relation to student and classroom outcomes. *Review of Educational Research, 79*(1), 491–525. doi:10.3102/0034654308325693

Mayer, J. D., & Salovey, P. (1997). What is emotional intelligence? In P. Salovey&. D. J. Sluyter (Eds.), *Emotional development and emotional intelligence: Educational implications* (pp. 3–34). New York, NY: Basic Books.

Raver, C. C., Garner, P. W., & Smith-Donald, R. (2007). The roles of emotion regulation and emotion knowledge for children's academic readiness: Are the links causal? In R. C. Pianta, M. J. Cox, & K. L. Snow (Eds.), *School readiness and the transition to kindergarten in the era of accountability* (pp. 121–147). Baltimore, MD: Paul H. Brookes.

Reschly, A. L., Huebner, E. S., Appleton, J. J., & Antaramian, S. (2008). Engagement as flourishing: The contribution of positive emotions and coping to adolescents' engagement at school and with learning. *Psychology in the Schools, 45*(5), 419–431. doi:10.1002/pits.20306

Rivers, S. E., Brackett, M. A., Reyes, M. R., Mayer, J. D., Caruso, D. R., & Salovey, P. (2012). Measuring emotional intelligence in early adolescence with the MSCEIT-YV. *Journal of Psychoeducational Assessment, 30*(4), 344–366. doi:10.1177/0734282912449443

Rivers, S. E., Tominey, S. L., O'Bryon, E. C., & Brackett, M. A. (2013). Developing emotional skills in early childhood settings using Preschool RULER. *The Psychology of Education Review, 37*, 19–25.

Tominey, S. L., O'Bryon, E. C., Rivers, S. E., & Shapses, S. (2017). Teaching emotional intelligence in early childhood. *Young Children, 72*(1). Retrieved from http://www.naeyc.org/yc/emotional-intelligence-early-childhood

Roberto and Maria

Two Children Dealing with Trauma

Families First Preschool, a full-day, full-year center for low-income 3- and 4-year-olds in the West Coast inner city of Santa Ana, tries to provide Head Start–like comprehensive services to all enrolled children. Director Martina Antigua, a bilingual Latina with a master's degree in social work as well as an undergraduate degree in child development, works long hours to creatively piece together multiple sources of funds. She is determined to provide a high-quality child-centered program with a staff to child ratio of 1 teacher to 8 children and an average group size of 16 in each classroom.

Classroom 4 is staffed by Latina Dianna Garcia, who has a newly acquired bachelor's degree, and African American Shavaun Anderson, who is working toward a bachelor's at night and on weekends at nearby Camarillo College, having completed her associate's degree over 2 years ago.

Through an arrangement with Camarillo College, Families First has five student teachers each semester, one for each classroom, allowing for the teacher–child ratio at times during the day to be even closer to 1 teacher to 3 children. Martina takes a special pride in this because over half the families served by Families First are headed by teen parents, who need the committed involvement and support of the teachers. With the help of the student teacher Anne-Marie, teachers Dianna and Shavaun are working more closely with 4-year-old Italian American Roberto Bruno and 3-year-old Latina Maria Rodrigues who are struggling with aggression and traumatized behavior caused by neglect and physical abuse at home.

The team of Center director and teachers also struggle to maintain good working relationships with the parents of the children. One parent is especially challenging since a court order restricts her from access to her son, Roberto.

"Why is he doing this over and over—he doesn't stop. And he's been doing it every day for the last few days since I have been here. Something very serious must be wrong with him, right?" Anne-Marie, a student teacher, stood with her back against the wall of the playground, her eyes wide and troubled as she stared at Roberto. Director Martina Antigua stood next to her on a warm sunny day in early October, about four weeks into the school year. She always took time to talk with each of the student teachers who came to Families First. She was determined that they would have the best experiences possible in order to assure that they would learn in-depth child development and early childhood education during their field placements, getting an excellent head start to their careers as teachers.

Both women watched Roberto intently. He was repeatedly entering the ground floor of a two-story child's playhouse. Outside the red and yellow plastic playhouse, a short arm's reach from the windows, stood a child-sized firefighter's pole. The pole was twice as high as Roberto, who with a strained, tense look on his face stared fixedly out onto the playground. Apparently he saw nothing, as he lifted one leg from the floor of the playhouse and, bending it at the knee, placed it on the windowsill of the small ground-floor window. Without looking at any of the children or the two teachers who supervised the play, he clambered out the window, stretching his arms out to clasp the firefighter pole. With his feet planted on the mulch of the playscape floor, he gradually lowered his tall body into a crouch. A quick look of relief flashed across his face. Standing up rapidly, he turned, walked a few steps, reentered the playhouse and repeated the exact same action. As they watched, Roberto repeated this circuit 25 times over the next 10 minutes. Over and over again. Roberto did this with the same tension in his face and body.

Glancing at him frequently, the two teachers in Classroom 4, Dianna Garcia and Shavaun Anderson, were calm, with no trace of worry on their faces over Roberto's behavior.

Suddenly, twisting forcefully away from the playhouse, Roberto strode decisively toward two large plastic, barrel-like structures that lay vertically on the ground, their wide mouths open in an invitation for the children to climb in and play. Reaching the first barrel, Roberto climbed in and folded his body over so that only the top of his curly, dark brown hair was visible to Anne-Marie and Martina. Crouched down inside the barrel, Roberto stilled his body and stayed silent for a few minutes. Then, standing up abruptly, he climbed out of the structure and darted toward the second barrel. Lifting his long leg over the top and folding his body in two, he held his face at a sharp incline downwards toward the dirt, his back rounded over, as he hid inside the barrel.

Over the next 10 minutes Roberto repeated this over and over again, his mouth set in a grim line and his face strained. Twice 3-year-old Maria tried to play with him by impulsively climbing into the wide plastic barrel, pushing him slightly to make room for herself. Each time, Roberto lashed out at her, yelling and hitting her forcefully. He screamed at Maria to "go away" and shoved her backwards, almost toppling the child. Each time, one of the teachers quickly intervened, urging him to be calm and pointing out a "calming down" area at the end of the playground. She encouraged Roberto to use his words to express his "big feelings." As they spoke with Roberto, both Dianna and Shavaun crouched down to his eye level and offered a warm embrace to him.

Roberto then returned to the playhouse, reentered it and began climbing out of the ground-floor window again, making several initial circuits. Teacher Dianna glanced at teacher Shavaun and gestured slightly with her right hand, as if to signal, "I've got this." She then sidestepped away from the tall children's slide where she had been supervising a half dozen 3- and 4-year-olds joyfully sliding down it. Shavaun moved rapidly toward the slide to take over and supervise those children.

Stepping toward the playhouse, teacher Dianna shook back her long black hair and placed her hand gently on Roberto's thin shoulder. "Perhaps you should try climbing the little steps up to the second floor of the house and sliding down the firefighter's pole from there," she said warmly to Roberto. Stepping back from his teacher and shaking his head forcefully, Roberto exclaimed, "No! I don't want to! I'll get hurt!" Folding his arms over his Superman T-shirt, Roberto fixed his highly alarmed eyes angrily on his teacher. He looked as if he would lash out at his teacher, hitting her as he had the children who wanted to play with him.

"I don't understand," whispered student teacher Ann-Marie to Martina. "It's not high. He'll be able to slide down the pole easily."

"Well," replied Martina, "It does mean that if he climbs to the second story of the house, his feet will be above the height of his teacher's head as she stands near the playscape. But I agree it's not high—I'll explain why I think it seems so frightening to him in a minute," whispered Martina, her body alert and her eyes fixed on Roberto.

Suddenly, her body large and plump, but positioned on nimble feet, teacher Dianna moved gracefully to the side of the playhouse, standing close to the firefighter's pole. She lifted both arms up high, curving them slightly and planted her feet firmly on the ground. "I will catch you, *chiquito*," she called out in her softly accented English. "I will be right here," she continued, emphasizing the word "right," her arms still head high as she smiled reassuringly at the fearful boy. "I'll be right here," she repeated softly but firmly.

Roberto hesitated, scrutinizing his teacher's face intently. Then he impulsively moved to the little staircase, climbed up the steps to the second floor, lifted and then lowered his leg out of the window and, grasping the pole, pulled his body over until he had two hands around the pole. He slowly slid down the four feet of pole, crumpling his thin body into a gentle heap at the bottom. Abruptly, he stood up, smiling, his face alight with pride. "I did it!" he exclaimed to both his teachers, grinning broadly. He rapidly and victoriously stretched up his thin arms in the blue and red Superman T-shirt, his dark brown curls glistening in the morning sun.

Roberto then turned and proceeded to repeat this action. He climbed the steps of the little playhouse to the second floor, out the window and, reaching out, scooted his body down the firefighter pole. Over the next 15 minutes, he repeated this action 25 times.

"Why is he doing this?" blurted Anne-Marie. "It is such strange behavior. I've never seen nor heard of anything like this." Twisting her body toward Martina, Anne-Marie scanned the face of the director, who responded, "We'll talk in a few minutes, but first I want to watch the teachers as they help all of the children transition from the playground into toileting, lunch, and nap."

Shavaun and Dianna walked around the little playground, ringing small bells, singing "Five minutes until it's time to go inside. Five minutes to finish what you are doing." Most of the other children smiled at the teachers, clearly getting ready to do what was asked of them. Roberto and Maria stayed focused on their own play activities and resisted the transition. Teacher Shavaun moved closer to each child, talking quietly about the need to get ready to go inside the classroom and the good experiences they would have there.

"Routines are essential for children like Roberto and Maria," Martina pointed out. "Come into my office and we'll talk," said Martina warmly, gesturing toward the door leading off the playground.

A few minutes later, nestled within two comfortable chairs in the office, hot water for tea heating up in the electric teapot, Martina leaned forward and said, "What I am about to tell you is exceptionally confidential, Anne-Marie." The young woman nodded, combing her fingers through her short brown hair. Adjusting her glasses, she looked at Martina expectantly.

"What I see Roberto doing is planning escape routes and hiding places, designed to protect him from harrowing situations. Several weeks ago, Roberto was abused—horrifically. His young teenage parents had separated, and Roberto was staying at the apartment of his mother and her 18-year-old boyfriend. His mother, Gloria Bruno, had to go to her night job and left him in the care of the boyfriend. When it was time for Roberto to go to sleep, the child cried and asked for a nightlight to be left in the bedroom. He's a very sensitive child and has a longstanding fear of the dark. Roberto cried more when the boyfriend absolutely refused, finally ending up screaming. The boyfriend, who had shut up Roberto behind the closed door in the dark, yanked the door open and, entering the bedroom, beat the child with his belt—including the belt buckle—and with his shoe. The child came to school the next day covered with raw, open abrasions and bruises from his forehead down through his chest and back. Of course, we reported it right away, as we are required to do so by state law—and by our own profession's Code of Ethics."

Martina paused, stirred her tea thoughtfully and looked over at Anne-Marie, saying, "The boyfriend is now in jail, with a fairly extended sentence. The CPS, or Child Protective Services, has been involved with Roberto's mother on the initial basis that she had not reported the abuse as soon as she saw her son the next morning. There's also considerable concern at CPS that Gloria Bruno, who struggled with alcoholism, needed both intensive support and close monitoring to prevent another incidence of neglect and abuse from occurring.

"Roberto's father has successfully obtained a restraining order, which prevents the child's mother from having any contact with her son for several months and then limited contact after that, on the basis that her judgment is impaired by her addiction and that she is likely to bring a series of boyfriends of questionable character into her life, endangering Roberto. Overall fitness as custodial parent for her child is being seriously questioned and she knows it. It's hard on her because she does really love her son," sighed Martina. "She has agreed to attend Alcoholics Anonymous and also go to her local health clinic regularly now to obtain medication and treatment. She's trying. She's only 17, and her life has not been easy."

"Roberto is not the only child here who has recently experienced abuse," Martina continued. "Maria, a 3-year-old in Dianna and Shavaun's classroom, was severely hit and shaken by Nina, her mother, as she dropped her child off at the door for school. One of the teachers saw this happen and reported the incident to Child Protective Services and to the police. They were waiting for her when she arrived to pick up her child at the end of the day, and I managed to get to the front door before she fully entered so I could warn her to stay calm. My own experience with situations like this is that if the abuse is not too severe and the parent stays calm and agrees to be involved with whatever the authorities recommend to improve her parenting behavior, then more drastic measures, like removing the child from the home, can be avoided. The police and CPS agreed they would require Nina to take a 20-week parenting class. Nina is really struggling with this parenting class, but she gets herself to most sessions. We constantly encourage her to get to the classes, and we talk with her also about positive ways to interact with Maria. We all see small but real signs of progress in her parenting behavior. In the meantime, Maria is provoking Roberto, just reaching out and hitting him as she walks by in the classroom. Yesterday, she deliberately tripped him on the playground, and he fought back, pulling her to the ground and yelling, 'I hate you!' at her."

Anne-Marie leaned back in her chair and looked thoughtfully at Martina, who glanced at the clock and stood up quickly. "Let's go back into the classroom," she said to Anne-Marie. "We can return here after we've had a chance to observe some of the routines that are being used to help the children transition through the different activities before naptime. For abused children, definite and clear daily routines are essential. They help the child predict what's coming next, which adds to their sense of safety in the classroom. For children who have not been able to depend on their parents for basic needs, the transitions from playtime to toileting to lunchtime and then to naptime must be handled just right."

Reentering the classroom, Martina approached teacher Dianna, and said quietly, "How are they doing? How did Roberto and Maria get through lunch?"

"It wasn't easy," replied Dianna. "They both fought with one another while waiting to sit down at the lunch table, even though we kept the wait very short. Roberto kicked Maria, and she just punched him back howling at him. Shavaun was in the bathroom, helping the other children, so I couldn't get to Roberto and Maria quite fast enough to prevent this. This is where Anne-Marie will be very helpful to us, I know," said Dianna, smiling at the student teacher. "Right now it's just hard to be in four separate places at one time. You can help us with the calmer children, freeing us up to give Roberto and Maria more focused attention."

Shavaun approached and, surveying the children who were bringing their sleeping pads out from their cubbies into their naptime place, said, "We've been talking with both children about the importance of naptime and how this is what's coming next. We know that for Roberto especially, but for Maria as well, getting ready to go to sleep brings up a lot of fears."

Dianna moved to go help Roberto, who was getting ready to hit Maria who had just bumped into him. As she walked across the classroom, she picked up a special device called a Mood Meter with its red, yellow, blue, and green corners. She had participated in special training led by the Yale Center for Emotional Intelligence where she had learned to use the Mood Meter, a simple yet effective chart with four quadrants, labeled angry, happy, sad, and calm. Kneeling down next to Roberto, Dianna asked Roberto how he was feeling and asked him to point to one of the four quadrants—angry, happy, sad, or calm. Roberto pointed to red for angry. "You're angry. Can you tell me why?" Roberto blurted, "Maria hurt me!" Dianna encouraged him to think for a moment about his feelings and to practice some deep breathing. As she watched his body relax and his face lose its angry expression, Dianna asked him to look at the Mood Meter again and point to the quadrant that represented his feelings now. He pointed to the green corner. "But now you are feeling calm because we were talking together and you're doing your breathing like we've practiced?" Dianna asked. Roberto nodded his head again, took another breath, and went back to retrieving his sleeping pad.

Eyeing him closely, Shavaun said to Martina, "Remind me to tell you more about his difficult morning as we made fall collages for the children's parents."

Roberto had made one collage with the other children, but before he could sign his name to it, he had ripped it up angrily, saying that his mother was gone and that he never saw her anymore so he didn't want to make her a present. Then he had made a second collage and had wanted teacher Dianna, who had sat calmly next to him, to help him write his mother's name on it. Then he had torn that one in two. Crying in frustration, he had crumpled up the paper and thrown it across the room. The other children by that time had put their art supplies away and were in the bathroom washing hands. Dianna had gently invited Roberto to sit on her lap, holding him and rocking him slightly as he finished crying. She had reminded him that whatever he wanted to do regarding the present for his mother was okay—he could either make it or not. Sniffling, Roberto had reached for the art materials for a third attempt at a collage for his mother. Once he had finished, he quickly made another one for his father, smiling. His teacher had hugged him, and with a relieved look on his face, Roberto had gotten up from the table and moved to the bathroom to wash up.

As Anne-Marie and Martina watched, Shavaun read a picture book about naptime to the children, and as Roberto joined them, Dianna had gently pulled him into her lap again as they sat on the floor. His eyes were frightened as he glanced around at the sleeping pads scattered around the floor. "I know you need to be near the door," said Dianna softly. "What will happen next is we will sing a few songs and then each child will go to his or her cubby and select a special toy or lovie to bring with them to their mat. You, Roberto, may select three books in addition to your special toy because we know that you need to read books to yourself to help you get ready for sleep. Let's sing the songs now, and I'll go with you to your sleeping mat and stay with you for a while."

"No lights out," whispered Roberto, "no lights out."

"*Chiquito*, we do have to turn off the lights so the other children can sleep," Dianna said softly, "But remember that there will still be some light in the room and one of us will be right here near you. We can rub your back if you would like. I have to go help the other children now, but I will be back."

As Anne-Marie watched, Roberto dragged his mat even closer to the bookcase right next to the door leading out into the playground. He tested the door handle over and over again. Then he reluctantly lowered his body onto his mat. He curled up into a fetal position, and hunched over a Superman action figure. His face was rigid until he caught the eye of teacher Dianna. His teacher moved close to him and smiled warmly at him, as she continued to survey the room full of children quietly getting ready for naptime. Martina turned and said to Anne-Marie, "I think the teachers won't need your help for a little while. Let's go back to my office, as it's important for you to understand what's involved in working with the parents as well as the children."

Returning to the director's office, Martina sat down in her chair and thoughtfully looked at Anne-Marie. "You see how important the teacher–child relationship is to children like Roberto and Maria. Of course, it matters for all children, but these children really need a stable and loving adult on whom they can reliably depend. And if they want it, they should have a gentle and warm physical contact with that adult. Plus you can see that the routines really matter, especially in reducing fears. You can see that both children are having trouble with self-regulation, the ability to manage one's emotions, attention, and behavior. Some children are more prone to difficulties with self-regulation because of their temperaments; others because their families don't function well and don't provide a home environment with stable, developmentally appropriate care and education, expressed through loving, predictable routines. Sometimes both temperament and family dysfunction cause difficulties with self-regulation. But inevitably, children who've either experienced or witnessed violence struggle with self-regulation—they are more prone to aggressive, impulsive behavior, and are often swamped by fears. I'm proud of the job the teachers do with helping Roberto and Maria develop better-regulated, more trusting behavior."

Martina went on, "Working with the parents—and grandparents—well, we struggle with that. Roberto's mother, Gloria, is an alcoholic, and she will insist on spending time in the classroom just as soon as the restraining order is up. But in the past she has shown up inebriated. Of course, we have to refuse her entrance. She gets very angry, yelling at us. She accuses us of trying to take her son away from her. She's distrustful and irritable, insisting that we have not done enough to protect her son from being hit by any of the other children. At those times, she insists on monopolizing the teacher's time, peppering them with questions about why Roberto is not ready to read yet. When she has shown up sober, sometimes she is warm and friendly and a pleasure to work with. Both Dianna and Shavaun worked hard to develop the best possible relationship with Gloria. And in many ways they have succeeded. Dianna tells me, for example, that she always tries to remember that she herself was once a teenage parent, and that bringing up a child when you're so young yourself is just really hard."

Martina got up and walked to her window and, turning, said to Anne-Marie, "Working with parents is one of the hardest parts of working with abused children. We come into this profession because we love children. Research clearly shows that the very brains of young children experiencing trauma are likely to be damaged, so that learning to focus attention on something like a picture book being read or a puzzle laid out to do on a table becomes impossible. And the very people whom the child depends on to feel safe often deprive the abused child of a sense of safety. Without that solid parent–child relationship, which helps to buffer the child against stress, the child is even less able to regulate the strong emotions that the abuse has provoked."

"How is this specifically affecting both Roberto and Maria?" asked Anne-Marie. "Is it that the traumatized child gets locked into the kind of rigid, repetitive behavior that we just witnessed? Without self-regulation, are the children likely to continue doing what we saw them doing today—becoming really aggressive toward other children, kicking, hitting at the slightest provocation?"

"Yes, to both questions," answered Martina. "Then it becomes impossible to make friends. Their whole lives can be ruined. Yet we, who really feel how unfair this is to the child, must continue to work with the parent in as nonjudgmental a way as possible. It's the only way to really help the child. That relationship is central to all the healthy development that we want for the child, now and over the course of his or her lifetime. But it can be hard, especially when the parent is really difficult to work with." And yet, the parents, she thought, were often trying to do the best they could with the resources they had. Gloria had explained to her that she had experienced physical abuse by her own mother—and that an uncle had once sexually abused her.

Martina recalled the many ways that she had witnessed both teachers being kind to the children's parents. They would ask each mother what she had done for herself over the past week. They would take pictures of both parent and child and then point out all the positives observed in their relationship. And they would listen to each mother, gently encouraging her to tell her own life story. It was during one of these listening sessions that Gloria had told teacher Dianna about the abuse she had experienced as a child.

As Martina reflected, teacher Dianna stuck her head in the door. "We've got a big problem, Martina. Gloria has shown up, despite the restraining order. She's been drinking again. She's pushed her way into the classroom and, sobbing, is trying to get hugs from Roberto. He's pushing her away. Then she's telling the other children they have to be friends with Roberto or she will tell their mothers about it."

"You've got to do what is required," Martina said seriously. "If she won't leave voluntarily, call the police. We have to abide by the restraining order."

"When we do that, we may not be able to work with her ever again. She'll be so angry. We want to maintain as good a working relationship with her as possible, both for her sake as well as Roberto's. She's so isolated, you know. Her own parents threw her out," explained Dianna, looking at Anne-Marie.

"And Roberto still loves both his parents, even after the traumas of the parental separation and the abuse. We need to maintain good working relationships with both of them," sighed teacher Dianna. Worry lines creased her beautiful olive-colored forehead over her large expressive eyes. Turning her head in the direction of the classroom, she said, "I'd better get back. But I just don't know how we are going to do this without rupturing the relationship we have with either parent and also worsening their own relationship with each other, which is so bad at this point."

Teacher Dianna sighed and continued, "His father, Anthony, is so angry at his ex-wife for having that abusive boyfriend in her apartment and leaving Roberto in his care. He worked so hard to get the restraining order. I agree it may be temporarily necessary, but Gloria is not an abuser herself. She has never abused her son. When she's not drinking, she shows a lot of appropriate warmth and affection to Roberto. I know that she can sometimes be irritable with me, but still she and I have a good relationship when she's not drinking. We'd planned to try and make a home visit to her apartment so as to talk with her while there's no risk that the restraining order would be violated. But once we do enforce the order—which of course, we have to—Gloria will be enraged and feel betrayed. Prior to Roberto's terrible experience, we'd had a good relationship with her."

Martina stood up and walked over to Dianna, gently putting her hand on her shoulder and looking at her directly. "We're just going to feel our way here and try to say and do the things that show her how much we do care about her despite her challenging behavior."

"I'll go back with you to the classroom, Dianna," said Martina. "This is a really hard dilemma—how to prevent her from seeing the son she loves because we have to—and yet still maintain enough of a working relationship with her that once this is over, we will be able to relate to her in ways that help both her and Roberto."

QUESTIONS FOR DISCUSSION

1. Experts in trauma assert that children's emotional and behavioral self-regulation can be affected by the impact of trauma on the developing brain. In this case, how do Roberto (and Maria) show specific problems with any of these kinds of self-regulation? Please give examples.

2. In this case, does the trauma experienced by Roberto come from one event or more chronic exposure? On giving your answers, think of trauma broadly, not only as physical abuse but also as other kinds of adverse experiences.

3. One of the contributors to the stress experienced by Roberto may be his temperament and specifically his sensitivity. In this case, what examples of Roberto's sensitivity are evident?

4. The Head Start Trauma Program (Holmes, Levy, Smith, Pinne, & Neese, 2015) addresses the needs of abused and otherwise traumatized children in the Head Start programs through a model that is designed to help three core domains impacted by trauma: attachment, self-regulation, and developmental competencies. In this case, how is each of these domains affected in Roberto's life? What are some of the actions that are taken by the teachers to help in each domain?

5. The Head Start Trauma Smart (HSTS) program (http://traumasmart. org/) provides support to teachers in four areas:

   a. Props and games to help develop attachment, self-regulation, and age appropriate developmental competencies
   b. Individual trauma-focused intervention, for example, play therapy, with follow-up communication to parents via home visits, phone calls, and written notes

    c. Classroom consultation to teachers and children, for example, recommending elements of classroom organization like a calm-down area

    d. Peer monitoring among staff and parents

What elements of the HSTS program are in place at Families First? If the program could be brought to Families First, what would you recommend as the most needed elements for the current situation involving both Roberto and Maria? Why?

6. In his article "Resilience: Where Does It Come From?" (2006), physician Bruce Perry describes four critical areas that influence children's capacity for resilience:

    a. Temperament (e.g., children born with a high ability for tolerating distress vs. those who are very sensitive)

    b. Caregivers who are attuned to a child's needs, strengths, and stressors—who respond in ways that are a good "fit" for the child

    c. Secure and healthy attachment between caregiver and child

    d. Opportunities and experiences that allow the child to practice mastery and success in meeting challenges in physical, emotional, social, and cognitive areas

In this case, how do these four critical areas manifest in Roberto's life at Families First? Please give examples.

7. The Adverse Childhood Experiences (ACEs) Study (Center for Disease Control and Prevention, 2016), one of the largest investigations of the later impact of early child abuse and neglect, surveyed and followed over 17,000 individuals. The study found widespread pervasiveness of adverse experiences, with about two-thirds of the participants reporting at least one such experience in childhood. Later life impacts included alcoholism, depression, health problems, and so on. In this case, how might Gloria Bruno's behavior as a 17-year-old possibly have been influenced by one or more ACEs? Should teachers become more aware of the ACEs experienced by the parents of the children in their classrooms? If so, how?

8. Renowned pediatrician Barry Zuckerman, MD, of Boston University Medical Center, who has spent his whole adult life working with and on behalf of children highly vulnerable to trauma, explains that the parents need most of all to develop a trusting relationship with their children's teachers (personal communication, April 2017). In this case, how do the teachers try to establish this trusting relationship? Do you think that trust can be maintained with Gloria, Roberto's mother? If so, why? If not, what can be done to establish as much trust as possible?

RESOURCES FOR DELVING DEEPER

Overview of Trauma

Kinniburgh, K. J., Blaustein, M., & Spinazzola, J. (2005). Attachment, self-regulation, and competency: A comprehensive intervention framework for children with complex trauma. *Psychiatric Annals, 35*(5), 424–430.

Zero to Six Collaborative Group: The National Child Traumatic Stress Network. (2010). *Early Childhood Trauma*. Los Angeles, CA, & Durham, NC: National Center for Child Traumatic Stress.

Impact of Trauma

Ayoub, C. C., O'Connor, E., Rappolt-Schlichtmann, G., Fischer, K. W., Rogosch, F. A., Toth, S. L., & Cicchetti, D. (2006). Cognitive and emotional differences in young maltreated children: A translational application of dynamic skill theory. *Development and Psychopathology, 18*(3), 679–706.

Center for Disease Control and Prevention . (2016, April 1). Adverse childhood experiences (ACEs). Retrieved from www.cdc.gov/violenceprevention/acestudy/

Chu, A. T., & Lieberman, A. F. (2010). Clinical implications of traumatic stress from birth to age five. *Annual Review of Clinical Psychology, 6*, 469–494. doi:10.1146/annurev.clinpsy.121208.131204

Felitti, V. J., Anda, R. F., Nordenberg, D., Williamson, D. F., Spitz, A. M., Edwards, V., . . . Marks, J. S. (1998). Relationship of childhood abuse and household dysfunction to many of the leading causes of death in adults. The Adverse Childhood Experiences (ACE) Study. *American Journal of Preventive Medicine, 14*(4), 245–258.

Grasso, D. J., Ford, J. D., & Briggs-Gowan, M. J. (2013). Early life trauma exposure and stress sensitivity in young children. *Journal of Pediatric Psychology, 38*(1), 94–103. doi:10.1093/jpepsy/jss101

Huth-Bocks, A. C., Levendosky, A. A., & Semel, M. A. (2001). The direct and indirect effects of domestic violence on young children's intellectual functioning. *Journal of Family Violence, 16*(3), 269–290. doi:10.1023/A:1011138332712

Kenardy, J., De Young, A., & Le Brocque, R. (2011). Preschool aged children. *Childhood trauma reactions tip sheet series*. Brisbane, Queensland, Australia: Centre of National Research on Disability and Rehabilitation Medicine (CONROD).

Shahinfar, A., Fox, N. A., & Leavitt, L. A. (2000). Preschool children's exposure to violence: Relation of behavior problems to parent and child reports. *American Journal of Orthopsychiatry, 70*(1), 115–125. doi:10.1037/h0087690

Helping Traumatized Children

Arvidson, J., Kinniburgh, K., Howard, K., Spinazzola, J., Strothers, H., Evans, M., . . . Blaustein, M. E. (2011). Treatment of complex trauma in young children: Developmental and cultural considerations in application of the ARC intervention model. *Journal of Child and Adolescent Trauma, 4*(1), 34–51. doi:10.1080/19361521.2011.545046

Buss, K. E., Warren, J. M., & Horton, E. (2015). Trauma and treatment in early childhood: An historical and emerging review of the literature for counselors. *The Professional Counselor, 5*(2), 225–237. doi:10.15241/keb.5.2.225

Cohen, J. A., Perel, J. M., Debellis, M. D., Friedman, M. J., & Putnam, F. W. (2002). Treating traumatized children: Clinical implications of the psychobiology of posttraumatic stress disorder. *Trauma, Violence, & Abuse, 3*(2), 91–108. doi:10.1177/15248380020032001

Cole, S. F., Greenwald O'Brien, J., Geron Gadd, M., Ristuccia, J., Wallace, D., & Gregory, M. (2005). *Helping traumatized children learn: Supportive school environments for children traumatized by family violence.* Boston, MA: Massachusetts Advocates for Children. Retrieved from www.k12.wa.us/CompassionateSchools/pubdocs/HelpTraumatizedChildLearn.pdf

Craig, S. E. (2016). *Trauma-sensitive schools: Learning communities transforming children's lives, K–5.* New York, NY: Teachers College Press.

Harden, B. J. (2015). *Services for families of infants and toddlers experiencing trauma: A research-to-practice brief* (OPRE Report # 2015-14). Washington, DC: Office of Planning, Research and Evaluation, Administration for Children and Families, U.S. Department of Health and Human Services.

Harris, W. W., Putnam, F. W., & Fairbank, J. A. (2006). Interventions for children exposed to violence. In A. F. Lieberman & R. DeMartino (Eds.), *Mobilizing trauma resources for children* (pp. 311–340). New Brunswick, NJ: Johnson & Johnson Pediatric Institute.

Heroman, C., & Blimes, J. (2005). *Helping children rebound: Strategies for preschool teachers.* Bethesda, MD: Teaching Strategies, LLC.

Holmes, C., Levy, M., Smith, A., Pinne, S., & Neese, P. (2015). A model for creating a supportive trauma-informed culture for children in preschool settings. *Journal of Child and Family Studies, 24*(6), 1650–1659. doi:10.1007/s10826-014-9968-6

Statman-Well, K. (2015, May). Creating trauma-sensitive classrooms. *Young Children,70*(2), 72–79 .

Preventing Burnout in Teachers

Abenavoli, R. M., Jennings, P. A., Greenberg, M. T., Harris, A. R., & Katz, D. A. (2013). The protective effects of mindfulness against burnout among educators. *Psychology of Education Review, 37*(2), 57–69.

Jennings, P. A., Snowberg, K. E., Coccia, M. A., & Greenberg, M. T. (2011). Improving classroom learning environments by cultivating awareness and resilience in education (CARE): Results of two pilot studies. *The Journal of Classroom Interaction, 46*(1), 37–48.

Resilience in Young Children

Perry, B. D. (2006). Resilience: Where does it come from? In *Children & grief: Guidance & support resources.* Retrieved from: www.scholastic.com/browse/article.jsp?id=3746847

Part II

CASES ON EARLY CHILDHOOD LEADERSHIP

Coming to Ground

The Leaders of All Our Children Head Start Agency Visit a Local Center with Problems

Individual Head Start centers and family childcare homes (as well as home visiting programs) belong to networks served by a grantee agency. In large grantees, anywhere from several hundred to more than a thousand children may be served. One of the strengths of Head Start policy is that it encourages "local option," whereby the federal government gives Head Start programs certain flexibility to design services that meet the needs of the children and families in specific communities. Creative leaders at the center and grantee level often seek and accomplish amazing collaborations that result in the braiding of many different sources of funds.

In addition, creative superintendents in the public school system, as well as principals of local elementary schools, often seek partnerships with Head Start programs. School districts may provide local prekindergarten programs by contracting with Head Start in order to provide quality services, since often one source of funding is insufficient to support quality. Counties and local private foundations often respond to Head Start and school system requests by providing funds as well, sometimes for direct services and sometimes for quality improvement initiatives like professional development, mental health consultants, workforce compensation stipends, and special curricula.

While these many sources of funding are welcome, they often result in many requirements, reports, audits, and, of course, numerous meetings. All Head Start programs must also comply with state and local licensing requirements in order to ensure that the floor beneath quality programs is one that keeps the children healthy and safe. Those programs that experience a serious violation of one or more of these licensing requirements are at risk of having their licenses revoked. In Head Start policy, when even one center served by a large Head Start agency has its license revoked, the entire agency enters a system called the "Designated Renewal System." This means that at the end of their current 5-year grant cycle, the Head Start grantee is not automatically considered for refunding, but must compete with other agencies in the area to obtain the funds to continue Head Start services. So the revocation of the license of even one center within a network of centers served by a Head Start grantee can jeopardize continued funding for all the other centers (U.S. Department of

Health and Human Services, Administration for Children and Families, 2014; Head Start Early Childhood Learning and Knowledge Center, 2016a).

As Head Start programs strive to collaborate more closely with public schools, they sometimes encounter problems with maintaining health and safety because public schools are typically exempt from licensing requirements. And as the owners of the spaces used by Head Start and other nonprofit centers, public school leaders don't always understand the role that licensing plays in the life of these centers.

Historically, Head Start has always offered opportunities (and some funding support) for classroom staff and family service workers to improve their skills and obtain better credentials and thus move up the ladder within Head Start agencies. One can often find center directors and even top leaders in large Head Start grantees who began their professional lives within Head Start programs—as teaching assistants, parents, and even as children in the Head Start program. Those who become Head Start staff manage to obtain better skills and credentials while putting in long days in classrooms as well as many hours per weekend planning; commuting by public transportation or traveling long distances in cars; running households; and caring for members of their own families—and going to school on weekends or evenings.

Yet given the very low compensation paid to teacehers, Head Start center directors face many challenges in recruiting and retaining high-quality teachers. As a result, they must also try to identify and recruit substitute teachers into the classroom. Staff instability makes it difficult for children to form attachments and this has a deleterious and harmful effect on the quality and even the safety of programs.

This teaching case illustrates some of the dilemmas that Head Start and similar nonprofit programs face as they try to balance all of these competing agendas and needs. It strives to situate these dilemmas within other more personal tensions that occur when leaders have to balance support and empathy for a colleague under stress with the reality that the central mission of the program must be preserved and whenever possible enhanced. While this case specifically focuses on Head Start, it portrays issues that are experienced throughout the entire early care and education field.

In this teaching case, Cesar Chavez Center is one of 35 NAEYC-accredited[1] centers operated by All Our Children Head Start Agency, a large multimillion-dollar grantee serving over 1,000 children in and around the large Rust Belt city of Carbondale, IL. The communities served are diverse and include children and families from African American, Latino, Euro-American, and Asian American backgrounds. As is the case with all Head Start programs, at least 90% of the children served at each center come from families who fall below the federal

1. NAEYC offers a voluntary system of criteria and standards that reflect widespread consensus within the early childhood field about what constitutes quality. Programs that are certified as meeting these criteria and standards are said to be "NAEYC-accredited" (National Association for the Education of Young Children, 2012b).

poverty level of less than $25,000 per year for a family of four. The area is rebounding from economic recession as high-tech companies move in; however, the scars of several decades of job outsourcing remain.

Cesar Chavez serves 150 children and is located in several portable buildings on the campus of Las Flores Elementary School. The school actually owns the buildings and rents them to Head Start. The co-location of Head Start on this public school campus supports the development of an emerging pre-K through 3rd-grade program, which in turn ensures that gains made by the children during Head Start can also be sustained during the first three years of elementary school and beyond.

Yolanda Ramirez is the executive director of All Our Children, and at only 50 years of age she has worked in early care and education programs for more than 25 years. She leads a team of 18 content managers (see Head Start Early Childhood Learning and Knowledge Center, 2016b) who provide expertise in the areas of early learning, health, nutrition, special needs, and family engagement to these centers scattered throughout the valley in which Carbondale is situated. She has gradually worked her way from being a teaching assistant with a high school diploma to becoming a leader who is currently working on her doctorate. She did this while supporting her family as a single parent. Currently, her two children are in college.

Sahara Alexis is one of two early education managers for All Our Children. Early education managers are responsible for supervising educational services, guiding curricula, program planning, and development training. They also analyze data and complete relevant reports (Head Start Early Childhood Learning and Knowledge Center, 2016c). Sahara has responsibility for fostering quality in more than 17 centers serving over 500 children. (Vanessa Richmond, the other early education manager, has responsibility for 18 centers serving about 450 children). Sahara has worked in All Our Children's classrooms for 9 years. Like Yolanda, she is bilingual, speaking Spanish as well as English. Both women have also learned a few phrases in several other languages including Mandarin. At 42 years old, Sahara still has three children at home that she and her husband are raising. She has managed to earn an associate's degree and is going to school at night and on weekends to finish a bachelor's degree and has almost completed her master's.

Going to school at night and on weekends has not been easy for Yolanda and Sahara, but now they are both able to bring a substantial amount of recent knowledge in both child development and early childhood education to their work.

Both women have held leadership positions at All Our Children for 7 years, but they have a history of working for the agency before that. As a Head Start agency that also braids public pre-K and child care funds as well as private foundation grants, All Our Children has a complicated funding picture and strives to comply with all the requirements that accompany this funding. Yolanda and Sahara consistently strive also to ensure that each of the 35 centers is

NAEYC-accredited. Working together with their whole team, they have brought the program to very high levels of compliance with the federally regulated Head Start Program Performance Standards (see U.S. Department of Health and Human Services, 2007). One of their proudest achievements is a QRIS rating of Tier Four for the agency as a whole. Not satisfied with that, however, they are seeking to raise the quality within each center to Tier Five. The Quality Rating and Improvement System (QRIS) is "a systemic approach to assess, improve, and communicate the level of quality in early and school-age care and education programs" (National Center on Early Childhood Quality Assurance, n.d., para. 3). A QRIS is established by a state and often has five tiers. Tier One is the lowest level of quality, and Tier Five is the highest.

Yolanda and Sahara endeavor to collaborate with all of the public schools that the children will be going to (as many as 50 local elementary schools throughout the entire area). Their vision is to work closely with the county office of education to help develop a high-quality, comprehensive, birth through 3rd-grade initiative for the entire county.

Despite their roots in classroom experiences as teaching assistants and teachers, Yolanda and Sahara have huge responsibilities that keep them at their desks and at their computers. For Yolanda, it is a constant dilemma: go to visit programs regularly or stay in the office to manage the safety and quality of what happens in these centers through the extensive databases through which she has access to so much good information.

However, solving the mystery of why one center is experiencing so many child injuries recently has propelled Yolanda from her office into a site visit to Cesar Chavez Center with Sahara.

"Lose our license? Impossible, Yolanda. Is that why we're heading toward Cesar Chavez this morning? That would be terrible." Sahara Alexis moved her brown eyes carefully toward her companion, Yolanda Ramirez, as they waited at the red light. Sahara kept her black-gloved hands fastened onto the steering wheel of the bright blue minivan on this cold, mid-December morning.

"I got a call from Benito Guarini in licensing this morning," replied Yolanda with deep concern in her voice. "The parent whose child was injured yesterday called the licensing authorities. She was really angry. She told Benito that there have been other injuries to children at this neighborhood center. I quickly checked all of our records, and I don't see any history of any kind of systemic deficiency that would lead to a health or safety risk. So I'm not sure what's going on."

"Well, we've never had a history of violations at Cesar Chavez. Never." Sahara again glanced over at her companion. "And under Helen's leadership we are making such great progress there. Several of the teachers are now at St. Mary's College and working toward their BAs on weekends. And the curricula that they're using now in the classrooms are research-based and have been proven to be really effective in both literacy and math. They are also using the Preschool PATHS curriculum for social and emotional learning [see PATHS® Training, 2011]. This has all just gotten started since Helen has only been there for 6 months, but it looks really promising."

"Even though we've never had any history of violations, Benito told me that they still have to investigate," replied Yolanda firmly. "So that means that we have to make sure we speak directly and honestly to Helen and make sure she understands that every licensing regulation requires careful compliance. I know that she's had training from us in this area, but she may have overlooked something. Every child's health and safety has to be protected as best as we possibly can."

"This is something we've always agreed on, Yolanda," said Sahara, her brown eyes glancing over quickly then returning to the road, "It's essential for gaining and keeping the trust of both the children and the parents. And trust is key," she emphasized, pounding the edge of the steering wheel lightly. "It sustains the relationships that allow for educational success. Helen's leadership around these good pre-academic curricula will succeed best if the parents have a trusting relationship and will then listen to the teachers and learn from them."

"I couldn't agree more," said Yolanda, squaring her jaw. "While we cannot protect children against every possible injury, we can certainly minimize the risk. And if Benito found anything substantially wrong and then if we actually lost the license for Cesar Chavez, it could jeopardize our Head Start funding for all the centers that we operate."

Yolanda rubbed her hand across her forehead and her graying hair in a gesture familiar to her companion. Her dark brown eyes stared straight ahead underneath her bright green hat, but her brow wrinkled with worry and concern. "I'm worried about this, of course. We also need to make sure that we keep moving ahead on improving the QRIS and CLASS[2] ratings for Cesar Chavez and those other centers. It's important for the children, and it's important for making sure that our federal and state funding continues to flow into our program." Yolanda consciously began breathing slowly and rhythmically, as she closed her eyes briefly, "I'm trying to deal with this through using meditation each morning."

"Good idea," said Sahara smiling, "With my three still at home, I definitely don't get much time for meditation, but I'm sure glad you do."

"It'll get better, *mi amiga*," Yolanda smiled back, "And then you'll miss them when they're all off at college. You're pretty amazing, you know that, don't you? Doing all this and raising three children." She lifted her coffee cup in a salute to her colleague.

"But maybe I should have started earlier," Yolanda continued. "There's

---

2. The Classroom Assessment Scoring System (CLASS) is a tool that practitioners use to assess and improve teaching strategies, which focuses on teacher–child interaction and assesses those interactions from infant care through 12th grade (Center for Early Education and Development, 2017). Pre-K CLASS has been adopted by the federal Office of Head Start as an essential way to measure and improve child outcomes.

so much to do this morning—preparing for the next federal audit, getting ready for the Parent Policy Council meeting and developing our agenda for our next meeting of the content managers. I know that I'm not always the best when it comes to time management. We're only 10 days away from the winter holiday break when the centers and the office will be closed." Yolanda leaned forward and pressed her free hand and her fingers against her forehead.

Sahara smiled sympathetically, "Oh, you're not that bad, Yolanda, I've seen worse in my time. It's always good to be aware of one's strengths and limitations. I have strengths in both time management and in building relationships, but I'm not always as good at problem solving as you are. You're always good at getting to the root cause of anything."

"Well," chuckled Yolanda, "We're going to have some interesting problems to solve. I got a call from the county office yesterday, and they definitely want to give us $15 million in additional funding."

"Wow!" Sahara interrupted, rapidly turning her head as the car swerved slightly to the right, inciting the driver beside them to honk fiercely, "Why didn't you tell me this before? Why did you keep me waiting? That's fantastic! I knew that they were going to find some additional funding, but I had no idea it was going to be that much."

"*Ay*! Sahara, don't get so excited! We have to get there safely!" exclaimed Yolanda. Turning her face toward her friend and coworker, Yolanda smiled, "Yes, it is great, *but* they want to make sure that every bit of it is earmarked for effective professional development for our teachers—and for the teachers in the public schools to which the majority of our children go when they graduate. That means a lot of collaboration, as you well know and that has to be done exactly right, Sahara."

"What do they want us to focus on?" queried Sahara. "I know that Elaine Wong at the County Office of Education is really interested in social and emotional learning."

"Yes, you're right," replied Yolanda. "Their highest priority is to support the public schools to foster better executive function and self-regulation skills. They want to fund mental health consultants and video-based coaching that supports better teacher–child interaction. But our team may not agree with this focus. Some of the content managers and the center directors want us to concentrate on early math and early literacy as well. And there's some interesting new research in those areas, especially for dual language learners in prekindergarten through 3rd-grade initiatives around the country."

Sahara glanced at her friend and said, "Well, there's some feeling too among the content managers that whatever new funds come into the agency ought to be applied to increasing wages for our staff, at least as a one-time stipend until either the state legislature or the Congress can better address this need for increased compensation in general. Some of our teachers are on food stamps because they can't afford to buy the kind of food that their own children need. It's especially hard for some of our teachers whose children have special health-care needs or who can't afford the housing in the safer areas of Carbondale."

"Well, we're going to have to speak truth to power, Sahara," Yolanda said dryly. "Our friends at the County Office of Education are not the problem. The problem is further upstream with the state legislature and even the Congress. Everyone wants to keep expanding early care and education services, but they refuse to recognize that we can't keep going on the way we have. We've been friends for 10 years, and we have good collegial relationships all throughout the county. But it's going to take some organizing to get people ready to speak out for increased compensation for our entire workforce. Fortunately, the PPC head, Maria Gomez, wants the Parent Policy Council to take this issue on."

"Is the county going to require that we meet additional regulations to qualify for these funds?" questioned Sahara.

"Yes, we're going to have to find a way to do that," replied Yolanda, passing her hand over her olive-skinned face and her graying hair with that familiar worry gesture.

"Well," said Sahara, skillfully maneuvering the bright blue minivan around a slow brown car that was creeping along the road. "There are too many regulations already, but we'll make it work somehow. As the data from our most recent assessments show, our children need better skills in several areas so that they can be completely ready for kindergarten. Last week in looking closely at the databases, I found some interesting things. It looked to me like my own classroom observations as education manager might be right. There's a root cause to why we've started scoring low on instructional support in CLASS[3] in some of our centers."

"Well, what is it?" asked Yolanda. Without turning her head, Sahara replied, "The newer teachers and the substitute teachers just don't know how to give good feedback by asking the kind of open-ended questions that you and I know promote cognitive development and good early learning. I think that this is in part related to all the substitute teachers whom we've had to recruit this year since so many of our teachers have left for better paying jobs as the economy improved. These substitutes just don't have the same skill set. They just haven't had the training."

Yolanda straightened her body and said enthusiastically, "The video-based coaching that the new funding may support will really help here,

---

3. The Instructional Support domain of CLASS assesses how well teachers are able to foster concept development through the quality of their feedback to children (e.g., a focus on learning process rather than memorization and on the use of analysis and critical reasoning) and high-quality language modeling (e.g., engaging in meaningful conversations in which teachers intentionally encourage, respond to and build on student talk to develop language) (Center for Early Education and Development, 2007).

and then we can more closely realize what we've always wanted—a truly high-quality program. The compensation issue—I'm definitely giving some thought to it, but it's a longer term solution. Still, I'm determined that, with the help of the Parent Policy Council, we'll do something about that too. This issue has been with us for far too long and things are just getting worse."

Expertly navigating the car onto the highway ramp, her dark brown Afro radiating out from her face as the morning light gleamed into the windows, Sahara looked thoughtful. Yolanda smiled, pulling her bright green hat over her ears, "We're getting closer and closer now to our vision for All Our Children. This is why I am so grateful that you were willing to accept this job as Education Manager." Ticking off on her fingers, Yolanda cited, "Nine years of classroom experience, familiarity with the research, knowing the Head Start Performance Standards, the evidence-based practices, the rating scales that we use like CLASS and ECERS[4], the systems that we use for monitoring compliance with our licensing requirements. . . ."

Waving her hand quickly in a dismissive gesture, Sahara interrupted, "Look, there's lots of qualified people on our team. Shelley, our East Carbondale family engagement manager[5], is really skilled. Remember what she did to help turn around those parents who were disciplining their children too harshly? It helps, of course, that she herself was once the parent of a Head Start child. She gets it—the stress, I mean. Will the county funds also support professional development for the family service workers as well?"

"Well, we've got to write a big proposal first, and it's got to be in by the middle of January, *and* we have to be sure we consult extensively with all the content managers. We also have to consult with all of the Parent Policy Council members and the Board of Directors of our agency, as well as the County Superintendent of Schools. And to really do the job right we should touch base with as many center directors and school principals as we can just to get their input. There are so many stakeholders here. I'm not sure if we should be even spending our time travelling to Cesar Chavez since it's so far out in the valley and almost an hour away. As it is, we're almost ready to close down for the winter holiday. Since this proposal has to be in by the middle of January, it means we've got a few weeks to get all the consultations and the decision-making done as well as to write the proposal and

---

4. The Early Childhood Environment Rating Scale (ECERS) is a classroom assessment tool that measures the quality of pre-K to kindergarten programs. This scale consists of 43 items, which assess the organization of space, time, and materials that support good quality interactions (Frank Porter Graham Child Development Institute, 2017).

5. The family engagement manager (or the family services manager) coordinates all activities at the grantee level designed to help families achieve important child and adult outcomes that are specified in the Head Start Parent, Family, and Community Engagement Framework (Head Start Early Childhood Learning and Knowledge Center, 2016b).

then vet it with the local public schools, who will be submitting their own proposal to obtain funds to then collaborate with us."

"You've made the right decision, Yolanda," said Sahara emphatically. Her black-gloved hands tightened on the beige wheel of the car, as she focused on maneuvering the small blue minivan through the encroaching traffic of morning Carbondale on their way to the Cesar Chavez Center. "You are making time to actually go to the center, talk to Helen and the teachers, and find out more about what's causing the injuries at this center. There have been four injuries in the last few weeks and three of them required ER visits. Yesterday Jamie broke his wrist and that's something we should avoid for sure if we can. Thankfully, the other children were not that badly injured. But I've been to the center three times in the last 2 weeks, and I've been shocked to see how stressed Helen looks."

Helen Stewart, the Program Director at the Cesar Chavez Center, had been hired 2 years before, directly from the state university where she had already begun working toward a master's degree in early childhood administration. At 25 years old, she didn't have that much classroom experience, but she had been well trained in child development. The same compensation restraints causing problems with recruiting teachers were also constraining the recruitment of experienced center directors.

Sahara had tried to coach Helen as best she could, but in recent weeks Helen had seemed more and more preoccupied. Finally breaking down into tears one afternoon, she confessed to Sahara that her mother had recently been diagnosed with breast cancer. It was hard for her to concentrate.

"Helen is under a lot of stress, that's for sure, and it's not an easy situation. But we don't want to restrict the children's play. When we renovated this center, we certainly did our best to have a safe playground and indoor classroom, so they should be completely free now to play," said Sahara. "I really want to focus on our QRIS ratings for this center and on increasing instructional support in the classrooms so I'd like to get this issue of ensuring safety quickly dealt with, which I'm sure we can. The two issues—safety and quality—are not competing. They are part of a continuum."

Yolanda leaned back in her seat and looked at her companion empathetically, "I know how hard you have already worked to try to get to the bottom of this. I'm not sure how much I can help. But since you really wanted me to come, at least I can meet with the staff during naptime and convey our vision for a program that is safe, healthy, and developmentally appropriate."

"Yes," Sahara replied worriedly, "I know it's not easy to make time to leave the office and actually go to these programs, but just your presence will signal to people that this stuff matters, and it will motivate them."

The two women spoke softly but with discernible stress in their voices.

Sahara sighed, "Look, we really see Cesar Chavez Center as a program that can move up the QRIS tiers of quality. It's only at a 3 right now, but they have good potential to move to the fourth tier at least."

Suddenly a red sports car swerved in front of them, and Sahara slammed on the brakes. *"Cuidado!"* shouted Sahara, *"Estúpido!* What is he up to? He must be going 80 miles an hour at least. He could cause a terrible accident on a highway like this."

Yolanda glared at the back of the sleek red car, while Sahara leaned on her horn, blasting the car that was now streaking down the highway, weaving in and out of cars. "Take a deep breath or two, Sahara," Yolanda exclaimed, "Stay calm."

Closing her eyes, Yolanda leaned back in her seat, her olive-colored skin paling under the strain of their near accident. At the speed that they were all racing along on this highway, they had just managed to avoid a fatal accident. She too began to breathe deeply, and she could feel her heartbeat starting to slow down a bit. "There's just too much stress in this valley, even with the economy beginning to substantially improve. Too many of our jobs moved overseas. Too much fear. Too much uncertainty. It's affecting all of us. We just need to be as mindful as we can of getting through this traffic."

"Look, Yolanda," said Sahara, training her eyes on the road. "I want you especially to talk with Helen, and I'll take over her duties while you do so. She may be able to tell you something that she's not telling me. I know that you knew her at the university when she was a student."

"I do like her, and I know she's got skills. And I realize she's under a lot of stress." Twisting slightly in the passenger seat, Yolanda spoke impatiently, her brown eyes glistening with determination. "But we *have* to focus on why these children are getting injured. And we have to prepare ourselves for the possibility that there's a serious licensing violation. We cannot risk a revocation of the license for Cesar Chavez. I sure hope I don't have to fire her . . . or put her on administrative leave. I would hate having to do that."

They looked at each other meaningfully. Two cars behind them honked their horns impatiently, and they realized they had slowed down quite a bit. Glancing at her rearview mirror, Sahara moved the bright blue minivan ahead quickly. Turning slightly in her seat, Yolanda said, "I feel we have to go to this center, not just to investigate but to motivate people by expressing to Helen and to the teachers what our fundamental vision and values are. We need to co-develop with her a good plan of action, which includes a focus on instructional support, early math, early literacy, social and emotional learning, as well as health and safety. I know that you have been there twice over the last week."

Twenty minutes later, they parked the van in the parking lot of the Cesar Chavez Primary School where the Head Start center is located. Shouts of happiness resonated from the outdoor playground where the children were climbing on the play structures. Two high slides were in heavy use as 3- and 4-year-old children happily climbed up the steps and slid down, their arms lifting joyfully as they slid downwards onto the mulch underneath. Looking up from the small sand area, Helen Stewart raised a bright pink-gloved hand in greeting. Against the chill of this mid-December day, a sea of bright red, blue, yellow, and green hats, gloves, and jackets worn by many of the children spoke to the care and love that they were receiving from both their families and their teachers.

Yolanda was shocked when she first saw Helen. She had put on at least 15 pounds in the last 4 months. Her eyes were weary. Her face looked strained and worried. They all knew how high the stakes were for this morning. Helen's blonde hair pulled into two ponytails that contrasted with the dark blue of her jacket, Her blue eyes looked very fearful despite the smile on her face. She approached the car as the two women got out and retrieved their laptops and belongings and began to head toward the center. "Hey, glad you're here. It's so cold this morning. We're going to keep outdoor play short. The children will be going in soon. Morning snack will be ready. And we'll have a chance to talk."

"Helen," said Sahara sharply. "That little girl. She's too young to be on such a high slide without someone right there." She pointed toward a small, petite Asian child with a pink and white striped hat. "You know the fundamental principles of active supervision for children.[6] No one should abandon their post at a slide or any high climbing structure when the children are playing. Not even for a moment."

Reddening, Helen's face clouded over and her eyes teared. A mixture of resentment and fear crossed over her face. "She's actually four and a half—she just looks younger because she's so small," Helen responded.

Yolanda reflected that this was not exactly the best way to begin their visit. Or was it? This was, after all, a visit about safety and quality in this center. Quality in teacher–child interaction depended on always keeping the children fundamentally safe. She decided to intervene quickly to bring the discussion back to as positive a focus as she could. "Helen, we know everybody here is doing their best. And it's not been easy this winter with so many teaching staff sick with the flu so often. It's been hard all over the agency. Sahara is right of course. But let's start our visit also by noticing so many of the things you are doing right. I can see for example, that you brought out the hollow blocks. I noticed that you've put a couple of used computer keyboards and some used headphones right next to them and that some of the children are already playing with these and the blocks in creative ways."

Nervously, Helen said, "Yolanda, I'd better tell you right away. We don't have enough teachers here this morning to comply with the Performance Standards. Two of our regular teachers called in sick with the flu that's going around, and I just couldn't get two substitutes in here quickly enough." Yolanda took quick action, asking Sahara, "Can you get on the

---

6. Active supervision is a best practice for ensuring a safe environment and the prevention of injuries in young children as well as quality: "The Head Start Program Performance Standards require that 'no child shall be left alone or unsupervised while under their care'" (Head Start Early Childhood Learning and Knowledge Center, 2016d).

phone right away with our office and see who they can possibly get to this center this morning? Tell them it's essential even though we are meeting the staff-child ratios required by licensing."

Until a substitute would get there, Yolanda knew she would not be able to have much substantive conversation with Helen, given that both Helen and Sahara would have to staff the classroom. Sighing, she decided to accept the situation and use the time to catch up on emails and to closely observe the environment.

Sahara took out her cell phone and moved quickly to the corner of the fenced-in yard. Yolanda turned to Helen and said, "Hopefully they'll get someone here within the next hour and a half. Vanessa, our other education manager, you know, just went to a job fair last week and got a new list of possible substitute teachers. And I heard from Vanessa that there's a course for substitute teachers being taught at Manresa College. We need that because it's been hard to recruit substitutes, given that in the holiday season people can get better wages by working in stores."

An hour and a half later, the children were happily eating lunch. While Sahara, the other teachers, and the recently arrived substitute teacher talked about the upcoming holidays with the children and what they planned to do with their families, Yolanda and Helen slipped away into a small, quiet office. Yolanda took Helen's hand in hers, "I understand things are pretty tough for you right now. Sahara has shared with me about your mother. How are things going for her?"

Helen's eyes immediately spilled over with tears. "It doesn't look good at all. They think it may have metastasized, and they're doing more tests. My father is just a wreck. I'm having to go over to their apartment every night as soon as I leave here, to help take care of her. She has to have special meals. And then I'm up late trying to make the lesson plans and preparing for the parent–teacher conferences that we always do this time of the year. And Shelley probably told you that we had a really frightening situation here last week. Last Wednesday a father showed up intoxicated with his son who had signs of abuse all over his back. He threatened to hit me when I said that we would have to report the probable abuse. We know this father and have tried to build a relationship with him, but he's just been fired from his job, faces eviction, and with Christmas coming up, he can't afford to even buy presents for his family. But it was really scary, Yolanda. Thank heavens the police came as fast as they did."

Wiping away her tears, Helen said in a strained voice, "I'm exhausted, Yolanda. I don't know how much more of this I can take."

Putting her hand gently on Helen's shoulder, Yolanda said softly, "Life does have some of these really hard times. You can count on us to be as supportive as we possibly can while you are dealing with all of this."

Wiping her eyes, Helen looked up cautiously, "I don't know how you can say that, Yolanda. I know there've been too many children injured here over the last few weeks. I'm just not sure what more we can do to prevent injuries. I've looked carefully through the Head Start Performance Standards, through developmentally appropriate practice, and through Caring for Our Children[7]. I've been getting up as early as possible to read them, trying to understand where we're going wrong. But I also have to spend two or three mornings a week right now trying to find substitute teachers who can make it into the center on such short notice. This flu is wiping everybody out including my teaching staff. And the children are sick too, and so they're cranky and irritable. Parents too. I think I'm failing you, Yolanda. I know you had a lot of faith in me when you gave me this position despite the fact that I didn't have much classroom experience." Helen's blue eyes welled up again.

"Let it go, Helen, just express whatever you're feeling," replied Yolanda sympathetically, "It certainly sounds like it's been tough." Helen broke down completely with those words and started sobbing. "I really want to do this job, Yolanda. You know, this has always been my goal: to be the director of a large Head Start center. There's so much good we can do for the children and their families. And I worked so hard for my degree."

After a few minutes, Yolanda leaned over and said, "Helen, I don't have much more time that I can spend here so we're going to have to analyze this situation as best we can. I must also tell you that I had a call from licensing this morning. They're coming to the center tomorrow to investigate. I'm not sure what's caused these injuries, but I did notice that the mulch underneath the slides was simply too thin and that's likely why Jamie broke his wrist yesterday."

Shocked, Helen said, "Does that mean a citation? I went with his mother to the ER and left a note for one of the teachers to rake up the mulch and go buy more at the store on her way in this morning. But she also came down with the flu and is one of the teachers who called in sick. I would have gone to get more mulch this morning but then with the two teachers out I had to show up to be in the classroom. I can definitely get more this afternoon. If we were to get another citation, it would mean we could possibly lose our license! And wouldn't that jeopardize our funding for the whole agency?"

"Yes, I know this is bad news. I also know that it's hard for you to hear this when you're already dealing with so much stress. But I have to be able to convey this to you." Yolanda leaned forward in her chair, propping her head in one hand, while the other gently patted Helen's hand, her brown eyes sympathetically trained on her companion's blue ones. "We have an obligation to the children, which matters more than anything else. More

---

7. Caring for Our Children is a resource guide for early care and education programs, which consists of "686 national standards that represent the best evidence, expertise, and experience in the country on quality health and safety practices and policies" (American Academy of Pediatrics, 2011, para. 1).

mulch should have been obtained right away. Perhaps you should have called a parent and asked for help. There's just no other way to keep the children safe."

Yolanda gestured toward the napping children in the other room. "We both know how much we love these children, Helen. We both experience such joy in seeing them thrive. And I know how hard you've been working to make sure that they do indeed thrive. Look, you're almost ready to move toward Tier Four of our QRIS, which means that the children are going to be much more fully ready for school. You've been doing so many things that promote positive teacher–child interactions. And the family service worers are establishing positive relationships with so many of the parents. So the kind of program that you have been directing here ever since you were hired has meant that the children have been thriving. It's only been in last few weeks that there have been these problems."

Yolanda spoke enthusiastically to Helen, but she also knew that it had been a hard year for the teaching staff throughout the 35 centers of All Our Children Head Start Agency. They had not been able to raise any salaries given their basic Head Start grant and the fact that state preschool funds had not permitted money to be used for staff compensation. As the economy had begun to rebound, precisely those teachers who had earned BAs with the support of Head Start funding were now leaving in greater numbers since they had their college degrees and could work in the public school system. And it had become harder and harder to recruit both new teachers and substitute teachers. Could this be one source of the other injuries? Yolanda reflected. Too many new teachers in the classroom? Too many teachers who didn't know the children well enough to know where problems might occur? Too little supervision?

Helen said defensively, "I'm doing my best, Yolanda. The public school owns these portables and Justina Truong, Las Flores' principal, doesn't have to comply with licensing regulations. So persuading her and her staff to fix every problem that could be a possible health and safety risk is really hard. They just don't get it, especially because the children are so young. They're not used to this."

Continuing, Helen said, gesturing with her right hand, "And then there's the problem of the substitute teachers. By the time the substitutes get here, there's no time to really orient them. We can't take time away from the children to do that. And they don't always know even the basics of what it takes to keep children safe. Yesterday, I was working on completing the monitoring reports, and by the time I got to the playground in the late afternoon, I saw that the mulch had been raked too thin by the substitute teacher. Before I could get it applied correctly Jamie had fallen right on his wrist."

Yolanda's mouth dropped open. "What? Where was that substitute trained?" She reminded herself to stay calm but inside she could feel her anger rising. Helen replied hesitantly, "Well, he was mostly trained to work in afterschool care for older children—that's part of the problem. He doesn't really understand 4-year-olds very well. He doesn't get it when it comes to either teacher–child interaction with such small children or assuring safety. He's just used to working with 10-year-olds, that's all."

"I'm convening a meeting in January, Helen," said Yolanda. "We've got to figure out a way to deal with this issue broadly throughout the agency. In the meantime, Helen, as much as I hate to say this to you, we're going to have to work with you to develop some way of enhancing your own skills so that you can focus on your work with the children and put aside your concerns about your mother when you're working here."

Sending Yolanda a grateful look, Helen quickly responded, "Thank you, Yolanda, for your understanding and for putting this all into the context of what's going on throughout the whole agency. It makes me feel better."

Sighing, Yolanda leaned forward in her chair and looking directly into Helen's eyes said, "We will have to do a plan of action specifically for Cesar Chavez very soon—like today and tomorrow. We don't have any time to waste. And I have to be completely honest with you. If we can't turn this situation around quickly, you'd have to be placed on unpaid administrative leave if a licensing violation was found. That's our longstanding policy." She reached an arm out to touch Helen's shoulder, but Helen recoiled.

"Well, that's not so supportive, Yolanda," Helen almost shouted. "You know what I'm dealing with, and yet you can still sit here and say that to me?"

Straightening up, Yolanda said firmly, "Helen, you know that Head Start policy will place the funding for the entire agency into question for the next grant funding cycle if a licensing revocation were ever to occur—even for one center. So I will work with you and Sahara on this substitute issue. We will get it solved."

"And while I'm certainly willing to listen—and, in fact, that's why I'm here," Yolanda continued, standing up and pacing back and forth across the room. "I want to also challenge all three of us to look into a positive and bright future for Cesar Chavez Center under your leadership. Let's get to work in the time that we have now writing down our goals and objectives for an overall quality improvement plan for this center. Let's think broadly about the Head Start Performance Standards, CLASS, QRIS and our school readiness assessments as well as licensing."

"I know you don't have much time because it's important to help your mother, and I agree with that. So I'll try and find a way to free up some of Sahara's time so that she can work with you and assume some responsibilities that will help you. Let's think creatively about volunteers as well," Yolanda smiled at Helen. Helen's eyes brightened. She turned a calmer face toward Yolanda.

"As we look over the next year," said Yolanda, pointing toward the elementary school a few hundred yards away, "I really want us to envision and develop a good plan for a pre-K to 3rd-grade program here, given that you are right on the campus of a public school. There's a really great opportunity for that. So we need to think through what it will all take with regard to professional development as well as recruitment and retention of the right people here at the center."

Helen sat forward in her chair and replied in a voice that shook with emotion, "I'd like to be able to do this, Yolanda. I really would. But I can't do everything. This is just the kind of thing I hoped I could do when I took this job, but if you can find me better support then maybe I can at least do some of what you're suggesting. But I recognize that I'm stressed, and I'm trying to stay totally mindful about the right kind of balance between work and family."

Yolanda raised her hand and said, "You don't have to do it all. As soon as Sahara can join us, we'll want to make a good list, which we will also use as a basis for helping other centers. This way you can be the leading edge of a whole quality-improvement initiative and not just a center that is struggling with the issues we've started to discuss here today. I know we can do this. We can continue to create a vision together that reflects our core values and start to develop a plan that will put all this into operation. It's a tough road ahead, but I believe in us."

Helen leaned back in her chair and looked at Yolanda with a mixture of wariness and hope in her eyes. "I hope so, Yolanda, I really do."

QUESTIONS FOR DISCUSSION

1. In this case, what are the primary issues? Overall lack of funding for early childhood? Lack of leadership and supervision by the program director? Inadequate preparation of the program director for her role? The contribution that inadequate compensation for teachers makes to the challenges involved in sustaining safety and quality in the classroom? The problem of finding well-trained substitutes? The stressors, both personal and professional, that affect leaders who are trying to motivate others and stay focused on a vision for quality? Any others? Using your own analytical skills, list what you think are the major issues in order of importance.

2. As explained in the Introduction to this book, one framework for the emotional and social intelligence that the leaders in this case use to deal with these issues is found in the work of the Collaborative for Academic, Social, and Emotional Learning (2017c) which lists the following skills:

   • Self-awareness
   • Social awareness

- Self-management or self-regulation
- Relationship management
- Responsible decision making

How does Yolanda Ramirez, the executive director of All Our Children, think and act in ways that reflect these skills? Do any of the other leaders also show any of these five skills? Why do you come to this conclusion?

3. In *Good to Great and the Social Sectors: Why Business Thinking Is Not the Answer,* Jim Collins (2005) describes five issues for leaders of social sector enterprises (e.g., nonprofit organizations), based on work with more than 100 social sector leaders:

- Defining "great" and calibrating success without using the metrics of for-profit business to do so.
- Achieving the kind of leadership that can get things done within a diffuse power structure, one that spreads decision making across swaths of employees. A diffuse power structure is not a hierarchical "command and control" structure in which an executive makes most of the decisions with little input and in which employees have little power.
- "Getting the right people on the bus" (i.e., the best team) within social sector constraints (e.g., financial constraints).
- Staying highly focused on three core understandings:

    a. What your organization stands for (its core values) and why it exists (its mission or core purpose).
    b. What your organization can uniquely contribute to the people it touches, better than any other organization on the planet.
    c. What best drives your "resource engine," broken into three parts: the resources of "time, money, and brand."

In your judgment, does the leadership of All Our Children Head Start Agency reflect the active use of these principles, both at the center level and at the grantee level? Support your conclusion with specific examples of whether or not Helen, Sahara, and Yolanda reflect these principles. Is it possible to develop these leadership abilities within the constraints of Head Start agencies that are also braiding funds from state pre-K sources as well as other sources? Describe the reasons for your answer to this question.

4. Holly Elissa Bruno (2008) describes the following traits as important leadership principles for early childhood leaders:

- Tell the truth with love
- Lead with integrity
- Develop partnerships so as to grow

- Be true to your deepest values
- Foster multicultural communities
- Be very curious
- Take care of you
- Let go
- Ask for help
- Find, use, and love your sense of humor

Do the leaders in this case embody these kinds of traits? If you think they do, explain which ones and why you think they do display these characteristics. If you think they don't, which ones do they not demonstrate? Explain why you think this. Would it be possible for the leaders in this case to develop all of these traits? If so, what would be the best ways for them to go about doing this? If you disagree that they would be able to develop all these traits, explain the reasons for your answer.

5. Mead and Mitchel (2016) as well as Derrick-Mills, Sandstrom, Pettijohn, Fyffe, and Koulish (2014) describe how Head Start and similar programs are most effective when they use data to pursue continuous quality improvement. Do you agree with the emphasis on the collection and analysis of data as a core emphasis in policy for these programs? What are the upsides? What are the downsides? Do you see any reflection of the issues related to data, monitoring for compliance, and a culture of continuous quality improvement in how Yolanda Ramirez, Sahara Alexis, and Helen Stewart try to carry out their professional responsibilities?

6. In your own experience as a leader, what have been the most challenging situations and scenarios that you have faced? What did you do to navigate these as effectively as possible? What do you wish you had done differently? Do you think that greater social and emotional skills would have helped? What would have been the role of technical expertise?

7. Yolanda tries to balance empathy for Helen's situation with a firm focus on the mission of the center: to provide safe, healthy, and quality early care and education services. If you were Yolanda, would you do this differently? How?

8. Both Sahara and Yolanda strive for a pre-K through 3rd-grade program as a way to ensure quality early learning from the preschool years through 3rd grade continuously at Cesar Chavez Center (as well as in other areas of the All Our Children Head Start Agency). In your experience with such initiatives, what are the major issues that leadership should address? How would the characteristics of emotional and social intelligence described above help? What else would be needed?

9. Licensing remains an essential floor to children's experience of a healthy, safe, and quality environment in all center-based programs. What has been your personal experience, if anything, with the value of licensing? With some of the dilemmas that licensing can create for programs, particularly in low-income areas? What do you see as the most valuable aspects of the ways in which Yolanda, Sahara, and Helen are dealing with these issues? What are the least desirable parts of their own responses? Would you do things in a similar fashion or differently to confront and deal effectively with health and safety risks? How does the establishment of a floor for health and safety work well to create an environment in which effective early learning can take place?

10. Leaders need technical expertise and a deep awareness of the laws, policies, regulations, and legal aspects of operating programs for young children. In your experience, what are the best ways to obtain this kind of expertise? What are the best ways to use it, especially when both time and money are constrained? Does technology help or hinder?

RESOURCES FOR DELVING DEEPER

Leadership

Bruno, H. E. (2012). *What you need to lead an early childhood program: Emotional intelligence in practice*. Washington, DC: National Association for the Education of Young Children.

Collins, J. C . (2005). *Good to great and the social sectors: Why business thinking is not the answer: A monograph to accompany "Good to great."* [New York, NY]: Harper Collins.

Kouzes, J. M., & Posner, B. Z. (2012). *The leadership challenge: how to make extraordinary things happen in organizations* (5th ed.). San Francisco, CA: Jossey-Bass.

Nicholson, M. J., & Kroll, L. (2014). Developing leadership for early childhood professionals through oral inquiry: Strengthening equity through making particulars visible in dilemmas of practice. *Early Child Development and Care, 185,* 17–43.

Washington, V ., Gadson, B., & Amel, K. L. (2015). *The new early childhood professional: A step-by-step guide to overcoming Goliath*. New York, NY: Teachers College Press.

Framework for Best Practice in Early Care and Education Programs

National Association for the Education of Young Children. (n.d.). Developmentally appropriate practice (DAP). Retrieved from www.naeyc.org/DAP

National Association for the Education of Young Children. (n.d.).[Website]. Retrieved from www.naeyc.org/

U.S. Department of Health and Human Services, Administration for Children and Families. (2016). Head Start Policy & Regulations. Head Start Early Childhood Learning and Knowledge Center. Retrieved from https://eclkc.ohs.acf.hhs.gov/policy/45-cfr-chap-xiii

The Continuum of Health and Safety as Well as Cognitive and Emotional and Social Characteristics of Early Childhood Programs

American Academy of Pediatrics, American Public Health Association, & National Resource Center for Health and Safety in Child Care and Early Education. (2011). *Caring for our children: National health and safety performance standards; Guidelines for early care and education programs* (3rd ed.). Elk Grove Village, IL: American Academy of Pediatrics; Washington, DC: American Public Health Association. Retrieved from cfoc.nrckids.org/

American Academy of Pediatrics, American Public Health Association, & National Resource Center for Health and Safety in Child Care and Early Education. (2013). *Stepping Stones to Caring for Our Children: National Health and Safety Performance Standards; Guidelines for Early Care and Education Programs* Retrieved from nrckids.org/default/assets/File/Products/Stepping%20Stones/Stepping%20Stones%203rd%20Ed%20updated%208-15.pdf

Assessment and Rating Scales

Fiene, R. (2002). *Thirteen indicators of quality child care: Research update.* Washington, DC: U.S. Department of Health and Human Services, Office of the Assistant Secretary for Planning and Evaluation. Retrieved from aspe.hhs.gov/basic-report/13-indicators-quality-child-care-research-update

Harms, T., Clifford, R. M., & Cryer, D. (2015). *Early childhood environment rating scale* (ECERS-3) (3rd ed.). New York, NY: Teachers College Press.

National Center on Early Childhood Quality Assurance. (n.d.). QRIS resource guide. Retrieved from qrisguide.acf.hhs.gov/

Teachstone. (2016). CLASS. Retrieved from teachstone.com/classroom-assessment-scoring-system/

Social and Emotional Learning

Collaborative for Academic, Social, and Emotional Learning (CASEL). (2017). Core SEL competencies. Retrieved from www.casel.org/core-competencies/

PATHS Training. (2012). The PATHS curriculum. Retrieved from www.pathstraining.com/main/curriculum/

Using Data to Improve Outcomes

Derrick-Mills , T., Sandstrom, H., Pettijohn, S., Fyffe, S., & Koulish, J. (2014). *Data use for continuous quality improvement: What the Head Start field can learn from other disciplines: A literature review and conceptual framework* (OPRE

Report # 2014-77). Washington, DC: Office of Planning, Research and Evaluation, Administration for Children and Families. U.S. Department of Health and Human Services.

Mead, S., & Mitchel, A. L. (2016). *Moneyball for Head Start: Using data, evidence, and evaluation to improve outcomes for children and families.* [Washington, DC]: Results for America, Bellwether Education Partners, National Head Start Association, and Volcker Alliance. Retrieved from www.nhsa.org/files/resources/moneyball_for_head_start_final.pdf

Issues Related to Inadequate Compensation for Teachers

Bassok, D., Fitzpatrick, M., Loeb, S., & Paglayan, A. (2013). The early childhood care and education workforce from 1990 through 2010: Changing dynamics and persistent concerns. *Education Finance & Policy, 8*(4), 581–601.

Whitebook, M., Kipnis, F., & Sakai, L. (2011). Professional development needs of directors leading in a mixed service delivery preschool system. *Early Childhood Research & Practice, 13*(1).

Whitebook, M., Phillips , D., & Howes, C. (2014). *Worthy work, STILL unlivable wages: The early childhood workforce 25 years after the National Child Care Staffing Study.* Berkeley, CA: Center for the Study of Child Care Employment, University of California, Berkeley. Retrieved from cscce.berkeley.edu/files/2014/ReportFINAL.pdf

Crises and Compassion

The Leaders of All Our Children Head Start Agency Use Emotional and Social Intelligence to Navigate Through Challenges

Contemporary Head Start programs are coping with a number of dilemmas. One of them is the tension between trying to allocate any available or projected funding to both professional development activities and improved compensation for their workforce. However, the allocation of Head Start funds is such that the average salary for teachers who hold bachelor degrees is very low, depending on the specific subprogram, (according to data collected by the California Head Start Association; see Mongeau, 2013). Teaching assistants and others are paid even less. Many other Head Start staff simply cannot afford to continue working in the program, and therefore program quality can deteriorate as teachers with whom children and families have developed strong relationships leave their jobs.

Head Start leaders are often torn. Loyalty to the program can be very strong, and Head Start leaders encourage this, but the Head Start workforce must also be able to provide adequate food, shelter, and other necessities of life for their own families. Consequently, leaders as well as the rest of the workforce experience a great deal of stress.

Simultaneously, Head Start programs must also meet multiple layers of funding requirements (as well as licensing) as they strive for quality services (see Case 5). Many Head Start programs also want to be NAEYC accredited. In addition, Head Start programs are often striving to move up the tiers of quality in the QRIS rating system and to score well on CLASS. As they do so, they also serve highly stressed families where trauma can be harming the child and potentially the whole family.

This teaching case illustrates some of these dilemmas and is intended to generate discussion about ways to cope with stress as well as possible policy-related strategies that would result in less stress for Head Start agencies. While this case focuses specifically on Head Start, the issues are endemic throughout the entire early care and education services field.

Like Case 5, this case is set in Carbonville, IL, a once-thriving Midwestern Rust Belt city now experiencing deep economic troubles. It is a cold, snowy, mid-winter day, and the 15-member, diverse management team of All Our Children Head Start Agency, led by Yolanda Ramirez, the executive director, is meeting for a full-day leadership retreat. They must make a big decision about accepting substantial new funds by the end of the day.

All Our Children serves over 1,000 children in 35 sites in and around the entire city. Carbonville was once a stronghold of manufacturing industries. Now many of the jobs have gone overseas and many families are struggling to make ends meet. Their children really need the quality Head Start services that All Our Children strives to provide. Over the years many children from Head Start have gone on to the public schools well-prepared for kindergarten, and now this agency has begun to intensify collaboration with the local public schools in a pre-K through 3rd-grade initiative.

The leadership retreat is being held at a lovely, light-filled conference center on a wooded hillside overlooking the valley in which most of the Head Start centers are located, around the heart of the once vibrant city. The Cassatt County Office of Education has offered an additional $15 million in private funds, earmarked for professional development of the teaching staff. The leaders are deeply divided whether to accept these funds or not. As an experienced leader who has served in Head Start programs for many years, Yolanda tries to respond to her team with a great deal of emotional and social intelligence.

However, despite braiding of state preschool funds and other private funds with Head Start funds, the challenges facing the agency, chronically underfunded like many Head Start grantees, appear to be intractable. Severely inadequate wages for teaching and family service staff result in serious problems.

The management team discusses somewhat heatedly the decision about accepting these new funds. Throughout the day, the meeting is interrupted by several crises reported by individual Head Start centers (not an unusual occurrence for many of their management meetings). The leaders summon up social awareness (including empathy and compassion), self-regulation (including mindfulness), and relationship strengths to solve the multiple problems they face. The leaders also briefly consider some policy remedies that would reduce chronic challenges worsened by low compensation for their workforce.

"No, we should *definitely not* accept that additional $15 million. I don't care how much it would do for the professional development of our teachers and our teaching assistants. We should turn it away. Just refuse it. We need money to actually pay the teaching staff and the family workers a decent salary and decent benefits—and we need that even more than professional development," Sahara, one of the education managers, stated forcefully. Her body stiff with determination, her brown eyes wide with emotion, Sahara studied every face around the conference table where the 15-member leadership team of the All Our Children Head Start Agency sat.

Her voice rising, Shelley, the energetic, intense, short, and wiry family engagement manager, leaned across the dark brown wooden conference table and brought her palm down energetically, "I do NOT agree," she almost shouted. "If we don't keep up the professional development of our teaching staff, we can't give them the benefit of the latest research on social and emotional learning, early math, and early literacy—all things that will help our children be ready for kindergarten and succeed when they get there."

As Shelley spoke, she pointed to a screen in this serene conference room where beautiful photos of young Head Start children were rotating through in slideshow fashion. Photo after photo of young children: some of them bright-eyed and brown-faced, with black curly hair painstakingly plaited into rows decorated with colorful barrettes; some of them with straight black hair, almond-shaped eyes and beautiful smiles; some of them with red and blonde hair pulled back in pigtails and ponytails, their pale skin and blue, brown, or green eyes in contrast with the bright colors of their hair; and some dressed in tutu-like, flouncy skirts with multicolored leggings on sturdy little bodies, their long black hair carefully tied up with ribbons, their olive skins and brown eyes radiating the pleasure of their play. All the eyes of the management team leaders looked in the direction of this screen, and their faces lit up as they did so.

In this hillside conference center, with its wooden walls punctuated by floor-to-ceiling windows that filled the room with light, these 15 leaders watched the faces and the joyful play of the children toward whom they felt so much responsibility. They knew that their work mattered in ways that could never be realized in other kinds of jobs.

No matter how they had found their way into Head Start and eventually into leadership positions, their love for children and families united them. They valued the comprehensive way in which Head Start and similar programs tried so hard to help families break out of poverty and sustain hope for children who would successfully move through primary school, high school, and hopefully college. It had been a good idea, reflected Sahara, to bring this slideshow where they could see it continuously throughout the course of the day. It was not going to be an easy day, given the complexities of this challenging decision about so much additional funding.

Malaya, the health manager, hesitated and cleared her throat. She cast her eyes down at the table, and then she slowly raised her head, looking at Shelley, clearly wanting to say something. Sahara noticed and said with quiet encouragement, "Malaya, I'd be interested in your thoughts on this." Malaya glanced quickly back at Sahara, shuffled some papers, cleared her throat again, and blushing, spoke up shyly, "I agree that more staff development in early math and early literacy will build on the good foundations that the teachers are developing with the children—who are already showing some good indicators of their learning successes. But since I cover mental health in addition to physical health for our agency, I am impressed that the county is also focusing its highest priority on social and emotional learning.

It looks like they're also willing to pay for mental health consultants. The teachers and family workers tell us as we consult with them that they are quite stressed by the challenging behaviors that some of the children—and that means some of the parents also—are bringing into the classroom. We need to listen to them. They are telling us that, without both mental health consultants and professional development in areas like trauma, we can't give quality services to the children or the families. Our staff members are burning out, and are quitting in increasing numbers."

Shelley leaned across the table and said, smiling warmly at Malaya, "You've brought up a really important point, Malaya. We really should accept these funds. And on a practical note, without professional development, we won't be able to keep up any of the scores on the rating scales that we need to comply with in order to keep receiving our quality improvement funds."

Pivoting in her seat, tall and thin Vanessa, the other education manager, looked angrily at Yolanda Ramirez, the middle-aged executive director of All Our Children, who had been with the program for 20 years and was respected by the whole team. Vanessa spoke up forcefully, glaring a bit at Yolanda, "We are friends, Yolanda. I've worked with you for more than 15 years. I know you are accustomed to my speaking bluntly. So let me speak candidly right now. You know that some teachers who work for us really engage with the professional development that Head Start offers and obtain degrees. Then because our salaries are so low, they leave to get better paying jobs working in the public schools. This causes a great deal of turnover, which is detrimental to the child and family outcomes that we all seek."

Sahara briskly stood up. She walked away from the table and then turned around. "We must have qualified people in place. Not substitutes who come and go. Right now, on any given day, we can't even get enough teachers to fill the classroom. I'm working 14 hours a day just trying to find possible sources of teachers and teaching assistants. I've talked to every single faculty person in all the community colleges and 4-year colleges around here. They've given me some leads—possible interns, students about to graduate, alums now at home with families but willing to work part-time, even retired teachers whom they know—but now I have to have the time to follow up."

Out of the corner of her eye she saw Vanessa check her cell phone and quickly get up and stride toward the window where reception was better. For an instant she thought Vanessa was trying to avoid joining in the conversation, and she could feel her irritation rising again. But she reminded herself that a call to Vanessa, the education manager, typically meant a problem was being reported from one of the Head Start centers. Vanessa quickly turned and said "Mount St. Mary's Center is down two teachers today. They've been trying since early morning to get substitutes, calling everyone they know. No one is available. I'm going to have to leave the retreat, Yolanda, and we will need one other of our management team who has classroom experience to leave with me. We can't fall below that critical staff–child ratio."

Yolanda sighed, but she looked around the table and said, "Helena, even though you have classroom experience, since you are the quality-assurance manager for our whole agency, I'd rather you not leave the retreat. We need your insights to make this decision today. You are the one who knows the monitoring, assessment, and other quality assurance data the best, and we need to base our decisions as much as possible on that data. That leaves Arturo and Nazila who also have classroom experience. Is one of you willing to do this, even though it means leaving the one full-day retreat we will have until summer?"

Adjusting her hijab, Nazila stood up and said, "I'll go." Shaking her head, Helena spoke up, "We need Nazila here. Yes, she has extensive classroom experience, but also working so many years in her family's business, she has those skills, too. Since she's been filling in for our former financial manager, we need her expertise if we're going to make this decision today." Turning to Nazila, Helena smiled and said, "You have so many talents. But we cannot spare you today."

Arturo spoke up, "Look, *amigas,* we've always worked as a team. That's what's gotten us through so many days like this. We can just help each other out. And besides, I'm the one with boots on," he smiled, as he pointed to his heavy boots. "I should be the one to go, just in case this snow keeps up all day." Glancing at her watch, Yolanda looked over at Helena and said, "I wish we didn't have to make decisions like this, and especially today. We are just short staffed everywhere right now. In addition to needing more teachers and teaching assistants, we need more managers on the management team so you all aren't filling in for one another all the time. It's been so hard to get good people for all these positions."

"Well, maybe we can convince Cassatt County to give us the funds earmarked for staff salaries," interjected Deanna, the Early Head Start manager, with a wry smile. Her dark curly hair glistened in the morning light as she sat closest to the window. "Instead of professional development, we could use the funds to pay staff more—maybe even increase our own salaries a bit too." A few smiles surfaced on the faces around her, as Yolanda reflected that good ideas come from all members on her leadership team.

Impatiently, Vanessa said, "Look, we have to go. We can't leave those classrooms in the lurch. And with the snowstorm it may take us a bit longer to get there." Yolanda stood up, walked around the table to where Vanessa and Arturo were beginning to move toward the coat rack. She gave each of them a hug. "We'll miss you, but we'll make sure that we send you the slides of the data that Helena will be presenting today. We will also take good notes of the discussion and send them to you promptly by email. If you can take a look at them at the end of the day just after most of the children have left and can give me your thoughts, I'll certainly incorporate them into our decision. Now go!" she said playfully. Arturo provided the group with a few humorous grimaces, an elaborate bow, and a little bit of fancy footwork as he moved toward the door. "Don't forget the party at my house tomorrow night. It's a potluck—so you all don't have to eat *my* cooking!"

After they left the leaders returned their focus toward Yolanda and the tasks at hand.

Sahara pivoted in her seat and fixed her eyes on Shelley and then glanced at Malaya, shaking back her long black hair intently. "No one wants to take these jobs when the pay is so low, even though we're doing our best to pay as well as we can and provide at least some benefits. We know we want teachers with college degrees and backgrounds in early childhood education—and we know that our funding requires it—but qualified teachers are not easy to find, at the salaries we can pay. This has got to change."

"We *can't* change that," said an exasperated Shelley. "That's a matter of federal and state policy. They won't *give* us any more funds to meet that kind of per child costs. And it's a shame because we can see that Head Start works. Our graduates come back to see us after completing high school, and even some of our alumni who are college students come to visit when they are on break. The policymakers understand that a good Head Start program is a great investment. And that's good. But they don't yet understand the terrible challenges that such low wages for teachers and family service workers create. So they only want to keep expanding to serve more children and to improve quality through professional development funding. Since we can't improve staff salaries right now, we can at least offer opportunities that might lead them toward degrees."

"I'm not so sure we can't do *anything* about teacher compensation," Helena said, turning to face Shelley. "I am increasingly concerned about stress and burnout in our staff. I spend a lot of time assuring quality by monitoring records and results on the computer, and we see lots of good results. But when I go into the actual programs, I see these results are achieved by teachers and family workers shouldering too much stress. Some staff live too close to the poverty line themselves. And some of them are not able to find affordable apartments within a 2-hour commute each way. I know there are some public-policy campaigns other states have launched to do something about this problem. Why couldn't we develop one of those here?"

"Are you kidding, Helena? When could we possibly do that?" Shelley stood up, shook her curly, red hair and walked to the windows, obviously trying to keep her anger in check. "We just can't take anymore. We just can't. As it is, we are giving up some of our weekends and even part of our holidays to try to make sure that everything is done to comply with all these different requirements and get ready for these federal and state inspections and reviews."

Yolanda Ramirez could feel her own irritation rise. Usually she could deal with Shelley's spirited manner, but today she didn't think she would have much patience for it. She knew that they just didn't have time for a lot of conflict. They had to get this decision made today, and there was a lot of money at stake. But, mastering her own feelings, she tried to focus on what was most needed to bring harmony into what was supposed to be a full-day team-building retreat for the leadership of the All Our Children Head Start Agency.

"Yes, this serious problem of such inadequate staff compensation has gotten so much worse in the last year or two," said Yolanda calmly, touching her brown hair that was streaked with gray. "We do have to do something about it. I have been reading research by the Center for the Study of Child Care Employment, at the University of California at Berkeley. [8] This problem of such low wages has persisted for decades now despite all the additional funding that has flowed into early care and education. I want to form a committee that includes members of the Parent Policy Council and a few of us to figure out if state and federal policies could address this issue better. Martina Garcia, the head of the Policy Council this year, wants to engage the leadership of the statewide Head Start Association. They want to see if there are some funds in state or federal or even local funding streams that could be used to increase salaries and benefits for all Head Start and other early childhood staff across the state. And maybe even the state legislature is now ready to take up this issue. The Policy Council wants to join forces with others in the early childhood field generally, to advocate for better compensation. You are right, Helena, there are other states where this issue is being raised, and people are much more aware that without addressing this need effectively, we will not be able to get the outcomes for the children and the families that all of our work is about."

Yolanda surveyed the table after saying this. Some relief was spreading across faces that had been previously tense.

"We will begin to address this, I promise you. I'm sure that the Policy Council will want to form a committee and will look for other voices to join in as well. Today, however, we do have to decide whether to accept these funds or not. Let's be sure to schedule a full discussion of the compensation problem and constructive strategies to respond to it at our next meeting with the Policy Council," Yolanda said determinedly. "We need now to get back to this decision about the Cassatt County's offer. This is a difficult decision for us to make. But I don't want it to split us apart."

---

8. The Center for the Study of Child Care Employment (CSCCE; [n.d.]) "conducts research and policy analysis about the characteristics of those who care for and educate young children and examines policy solutions aimed at improving how our nation prepares, supports, and rewards these early educators to ensure young children's optimal development. . . . CSCCE also works directly with policymakers and a range of national, state, and local organizations to assess policy proposals and provide technical assistance on implementing sound early care and education workforce policy" (para. 1).

As she talked, Yolanda was also reflecting that, over the years, her leadership group had managed to get through many challenges by working together as a team. Now she was concerned that team building would fail because of these fractious issues. Leaning forward in her leather chair, her hands resting firmly on the gleaming brown table, her eyes steady, she said, "I think we should go around the room and express not just our opinions about what decision we should make and why, but our feelings and emotions as well. Our teachers and family service workers are not the only ones who are stressed. We are too. We've just come through the winter holidays and all the accountability-related performance reviews for compliance that we had just before the holidays—and the ones we now have to get ready for. We can't just expect to deal with all of the emotion that this engenders without being able to express it a bit. Do you all agree?"

Yolanda looked around the room at the 15 weary faces in front of her. She knew that she had to motivate the leadership team not just to get through the difficult decision that they had to make during this full day staff retreat but to rise to even greater levels of leadership. Some might argue that just getting the problem solved about whether to take the additional funds being offered was all that the group needed to accomplish today. But she knew that she needed to take them to their shared commitment, which would continue to motivate them. Could she do it again, when they were all so tired?

So she stood up and walked slowly down the side of the conference table nearest the floor-to-ceiling windows that shed so much light into the room, her brown eyes looking intently at each face as she did so. "You know we have such a good record of success for so many of the children who have gone to our program. There are so many children who have graduated from high school, gone on to college, and are working, some of them even in those new tech companies that are trying to establish themselves now in the Valley. Last year we had even more children showing good school readiness skills on our assessment protocol. And we are enrolling more babies and parents in Early Head Start. And don't forget that we are also helping the children sustain the gains that they are making in Head Start. Last year we collaborated more effectively with more school districts in order to work with the children until they are at least reading and doing math well by the end of 3rd grade. We know that's going to mean even greater success as they move through school. Our children are going to succeed in school and in life!"

The faces brightened. This was why everyone did this work, of course. It was a great group of human beings, Yolanda knew, really dedicated and committed. She could feel inside herself the resolve to rise above the many challenges and articulate their common vision of better lives for the children and families.

Yolanda thought back to the leadership institutes that she had attended over the years. Often, they had focused on the technical and policy aspects of governance and other important issues. But they had also emphasized vision and a leader's responsibility for articulating her vision well. And the agency's mental health consultant also stressed the importance of emotionally and socially intelligent leadership. The consultant often said that until they could get adequate funding to really reflect the true cost of their program, they had to make a concerted effort to master all the stress in their lives. Yolanda strove to accomplish this, but also continued to struggle with her doubts about her own leadership abilities.

She sighed, saying, "Everywhere in this country there is now recognition of the value of investing in good-quality early childhood education. We all know that the work of the teaching and family service staff creates whole new developmental pathways for the children and their parents—pathways that lead to greater economic self-sufficiency, improved parenting, completely different life outcomes. We can now begin to dream of a day where every early childhood classroom will be staffed not only by qualified and dedicated teachers, but also by those who are well-compensated so they can afford to commit themselves to our program for many years. Same for the family service staff. That day will come. We'll be able to walk into any classroom and see strong bonds between teachers and children and the effective instruction that is grounded in those relationships."

"Things will get better. It took decades of work to get us to this point—things move slowly at the policy level but because I've been in the field for so long, I can see that we are almost now at a tipping point. We do have to reduce the stress on the teachers and family service workers—and on ourselves. But the time will come when we can get this job done with significantly less stress."

Pulling back slightly, Yolanda realized that right now she would need to recognize her own stress and fears. She was going to have to lead the agency through a series of crises that they would be facing as they went further into the wintry months in this sprawling, cold midwestern city. Anxiously, she glanced outside. On the other side of the full-length glass windows in this remote conference center, the snow had begun to fall. There had been predictions for a blizzard but it wasn't supposed to start until the weekend. She would need to get the managers home early if the snow piled up too rapidly. And they still had a lot to get through on their agenda.

"So let's spend a few minutes just voicing some of our feelings. And those of you who want to can also speak about the constructive strategies you are using to deal with them—or you can even say what you would want to have changed in our agency." said Yolanda in a warm persuasive voice.

The leaders glanced at one another, and nobody spoke for a few minutes. Then Deanna said quietly, "I know that I'm just scared. I know that that's what I'm feeling. I'm just not sure we can do all this, Yolanda. There's only 24 hours in a day. I love this Early Head Start job. I love seeing these babies and toddlers thriving. But I find myself going to bed later and later each night. And some nights, I have trouble falling asleep. There's so much to worry about. I am using a meditation podcast that I found and that does help a bit. I feel that if I can keep trying I'll get better at this. But some nights I just can't stop the worry, I just can't seem to help myself."

"I'm really glad that you brought this up, Deanna," said Yolanda in a quiet voice, which she hoped might have a calming effect on others. "I know that I've had a few sleepless nights myself, and I'm trying to understand better what I can do about it and what all of us can do to reduce the stress that we're feeling. I also use meditation; perhaps we can share our podcasts," she said, smiling at Deanna.

Suddenly, Malaya, usually so quiet during the leadership team meetings, bursts out, "Well, I sleep okay, but my family says that they never get to see me anymore. I have three children and as much as I care about the children and the families that we serve, I can't neglect my own family." There were nods of agreement around the table.

Yolanda began to debate within herself. Was this going to turn out to be just a venting session? A gripe session? The mental health consultant she communicated with as she prepared for this full-day retreat encouraged her to focus on the leaders' feelings and not just on getting decisions made. And she knew that this decision about the additional $15 million in funding had to be made by the end of the day, but it was not going to be easy. If they turned away the funds, the county might decide to provide the funds to another organization. There were, after all, other agencies in the community serving low-income children and families. And she knew that the teaching staff could dearly use some good professional development about challenging behaviors. Their survey data had shown marked desire on the part of teaching staff and family workers for such help.

"No," she thought. "We need more of this team building. The problems are too big and too constant. None of us can feel isolated within our own distinct responsibilities, whether it's for early learning, health services, family engagement, special needs children, even facilities or recruitment and enrollment. We have to be willing to have those courageous conversations about our worries and concerns and be able to expose our vulnerabilities to one another in order to plan well and come up with the best possible strategies."

Yolanda turned back to the group with renewed confidence in herself. She reflected wryly that those skills in self-regulation, mindfulness, and calm problem-solving approaches that she had learned over the years from mindfulness meditation had been invaluable in ways that she hadn't originally envisioned. She had developed a greater self-awareness that led to a better understanding of both her own strengths and limitations. She had been encouraging the leaders to consider using these strategies as well, and some were starting to do so. Her long-term vision was that someday the teachers would use mindfulness in their work with children and parents.

The research showed that this could enhance focus and compassion, both of which were essential to solving the problems at hand. Yolanda had taken a course on emotional and social intelligence in leadership which had propelled her to better use of skills for self-regulation, mindfulness, and calm problem solving.

Like many early childhood educators, she had gone into that course with well-developed skills in working with children. And over the years she had worked at building her skills for interacting with adults as well; first with parents, teachers, and coaches when she had been a program director of a center with many classrooms. Therefore, she came into this job with strong social skills, including the cultural and linguistic awareness that was so important to working in a multicultural program. Over the years she had learned a lot about relationship building and maintenance. But, like many other early childhood educators, she was more aware of others' needs than her own. And she had focused more on her limitations, and was less aware of her strengths.

Yolanda had systematically worked at developing self-awareness skills, using daily mindfulness meditation to calm her mind and look at what was truly causing her to feel stressed. So now she knew that her own fears were holding her back from spending an hour listening to the fears and worries of her leadership team. They would need to do at least some of this before they could move on to analyze the problem well and develop both the strategies and the courage to advance further the solutions that looked most promising. She wondered if they could persuade the Cassatt County Office of Education staff to provide some of the funds for staff compensation increases, which would reduce one big source of stress.

In the meantime, the leaders would need to express their feelings about the full range of issues with which they were dealing. Yolanda knew that Shelley, who liked to make decisions quickly, would object to spending time on this, and that even Vanessa would want to move quickly on to dealing with the major decision for today, but Yolanda knew that she needed to convince them to try.

"Everything we say today, let's keep confidential among ourselves." She rose and went to the whiteboard. "Let's just spend a few minutes listing the concerns that we have. Then we will move on to thoroughly analyzing this issue and developing the best possible response. If we take these steps, we will have done our best which is all that we can hope to do."

"Okay, down to business," said Yolanda firmly. "The proposal that we submitted to the Cassatt Office of Education is in your binders, along with their notice of the award to us. Malaya, can you take notes on the whiteboard? Helena, would you be sure to see to it that you take some notes on your laptop so we can send them quickly to Arturo and Vanessa? Who wants to go first with listing some of the positive reasons why we should accept these funds?"

"Well, I can go first," Shelley chimed in, "and I've been thinking about what has been discussed here. There does need to be an advocacy strategy, and I think we should develop a Plan B here that would allow us to go back to the county and explain that we would want to see at least part of these funds be directed toward workforce compensation. We have good data that would substantiate this need."

"We can explain why this matters by describing the problem with using so many substitute teachers since we can't pay well enough to recruit and retain regular teachers," Shelley continued. "You recall, Sahara, that in December we came close to losing our license for the Cesar Chavez Center because there were so many injuries there, partly due to using substitute teachers who were not trained in early childhood care. In addition, many of our centers are dealing with traumatized children. We've just come through the winter holidays, and as you know, it's a time that can be very stressful for families—especially those who are working several jobs because of seasonal employment in the stores and elsewhere. Some families have been so affected by the stressors that children have shown up at our centers abused."

"Yes, that's true," said Sahara, "And as you know very well, Shelley, substitute teachers cannot really engage with the families. There needs to be continuity in those relationships too. Continuity in relationships with young children is so important. But relationships matter a great deal to families as well. And substitute teachers don't develop those relationships that really can help when families come under a lot of stress."

"Yes, we have to connect the dots here; we have to do more of a systems analysis," said Deanna. "You are right, Shelley. This problem isn't just about substitute teachers and their inability to really help stressed families. That's serious enough. But not being able to keep our regular teachers working in Head Start, especially after they've earned their BAs when they can get paid better by the public schools, is connected to all of this. And that in turn means that not only can we not help traumatized children and stressed families well, we can't achieve the outcomes that every funding source is expecting us to achieve. Something has to change."

Yolanda squirmed impatiently in her seat. "I agree. But it's now almost lunchtime, and we haven't really had a full discussion yet on this decision that we have to make today. We should discuss this issue of substitute teachers in some depth at our next monthly meeting. If we could agree to that, I would then feel more relieved and able to focus better. I need to know that we can resolve today the issue of whether or not to accept the $15 million in new funding."

The managers looked at one another and then nodded. Shelley stood up and strode to the whiteboard. "I'm ready," she said. Yolanda looked at each face to make sure that they were really ready—their minds focused on the task at hand and not on the different problems that they'd already had to solve this morning. And then she said, "Okay, let's start with the data that

Helena has for us today in her presentation, and then we will proceed to brainstorming the pros and cons; after analyzing those, we'll be better able to make our decision."

Two hours later, after the database presentation by Helena and the brainstorming session, the whiteboard was filled with writing. And there were large pieces of paper taped to the walls as well, containing different opinions—pros and cons—the reasons for them, and the financial and managerial systems that would need to be put into place. They had worked effectively together and were close to making a decision now.

The snow was piling up, and although the issue was not yet quite resolved, Yolanda and her team knew that they would undoubtedly have to leave early if they were going to avoid getting stuck in hours of traffic crawling slowly across the freeway. The leaders knew that their own children's care arrangements would have to close much earlier than usual. No one wanted to be so late that they were making teachers at other programs wait hours for them to show up.

"I think we are ready to start synthesizing what we have just discussed and creating a couple of summary paragraphs, so that we can send them to Arturo and Vanessa." Within 20 minutes, the paragraphs synthesizing the discussion were on their way to Arturo and Vanessa.

The managers turned back to the issue of developing a more data-based way of monitoring the performance of substitute teachers that they now had to recruit into the classrooms, while they waited to hear back from Vanessa and Arturo. They knew that, even if they had the time to quickly go over the emailed notes, it would be at least another hour of discussion after that, before they could come up with the best possible plan. There would be so many follow-up items to be organized before early next week. But they also needed to go home—and soon. Snow was piling up and their long commutes would be highly stressful.

It had been a challenging day, but they could feel the strength of their relationships with one another—always such a positive elements of their leadership efforts together.

Yolanda sat back in her chair and reflected on the day. She wondered what would be the final decision. What would this group of committed and dedicated individuals decide to do about this new funding?

QUESTIONS FOR DISCUSSION

1. In this case, what do you feel are the primary issues: A difficult decision involving extra funds that will address some of the agency's needs but not others and will carry with it additional layers of quality assurance requirements? The stress that the leadership team experiences, both chronically and acutely on this particular day? The teacher shortage

and the subsequent hunt for both new teachers and substitute teachers? The problem of low compensation for the teachers and teaching assistants? Any others? Using your own analytical skills, list what *you* think are the major issues, in the order in which you think they are most important.

2. Goleman, Boyatzis, and McKee (2002) state that effective leaders have resonance, which boosts performance. They describe four styles of resonant leadership:

    a. Visionary (motivating people toward shared dreams)
    b. Coaching (connecting the desires of a person with the organization's goals)
    c. Affiliative (creating harmonious relationships by connecting people to each other)
    d. Democratic (valuing people's input and eliciting commitment through participation)

    This framework also involves characteristics such as empathy and motivation. Do both Yolanda Ramirez and the other leaders in this case show behaviors that would be compatible with the framework by Goleman et al.? Explain why you think so and why this framework might be an alternative way of understanding the emotionally and socially intelligent behaviors of leaders.

3. In this case, how does the use of these emotionally and socially intelligent behaviors contribute to the discussions and decisions that the leaders undertake as they deal with what you feel are the primary issues presented in the case?

4. In this case, are there policy solutions to some of these issues that are discussed, even briefly? To discuss this query as it relates to inadequate workforce compensation, the research by Whitebook, Phillips, and Howes (2014) will give important information and insights into how this severe problem has persisted, how it dramatically constrains our efforts at sustaining and improving quality, and how it both needs to be and can be changed by some valuable policy solutions.

5. The work of Washington, Gadson, and Amel (2015) lays out 11 interconnected steps for leaders becoming architects of change:

    a. Face reality
    b. Respect our own knowledge
    c. Recognize our experiences of isolation, intimidation, and negation by others (symptoms of conflict where others have more power than we do)
    d. Carefully make the decision to advance toward solving a hard issue—or to retreat from that path

   e. Know our own vision and identity and connect to one another and
      our profession to realize our vision
   f. Share strategies and leadership through a confidential community
      that encourages one another
   g. Begin with reflection on the issues we face everyday
   h. Use what we know everyday to align what we know to what we ac-
      tually do in every situation
   i. Focus on what we do want, not what we don't want
   j. Gather our allies among colleagues, friends, and supervisors
   k. Document and communicate impact, especially through our stories

   In this case, do the leaders display some of the characteristics of leadership and leader behavior that Washington et al. describe and document?
   List which ones you think they do. List those behaviors that are not
   reflected by the behavior of the leaders in this case. Which of these behaviors would you consider most important for effective leadership of a
   large Head Start agency or a similar program?

6. Derrick-Mills, Sandstrom, Pettijohn, Fyffe, and Koulish (2014), who
   have studied leadership as it relates to a data-based approach for continuous quality improvement in Head Start, describe three characteristics of effective leaders who do use data for decision-making. Effective
   leaders must:

   • Be strong, committed, inclusive, and participatory
   • Have strong analytic capacity and skills
   • Focus on priorities and commit time and resources well
   • Create an organizational culture of learning, including creating safe
     spaces for difficult discussions

   In this case, how do the leaders of All Our Children display some of
   these cognitive and other skills that complement well their emotionally
   and socially intelligent skills?

7. Nicholson and Kroll (2014) describe a process of inquiry by which professionals can develop a deeper understanding of leadership through ex-
   amination of a specific "dilemma of professional practice." This process
   involves "sharing without interruption, careful listening, self-reflection,
   and description versus evaluation," which allows for conflicting perspectives to be voiced and permits leaders to guide the discussion participants
   to "expand their perspectives and develop more equitable and just professional practice" (p. 2). In this case, do these leaders exemplify the process
   laid out by Nicholson and Kroll? Where in the discussion carried out in
   this case do they display some of these principles? Where do they not?
   Give specific examples as you voice your response to this query.

8. Yolanda Ramirez strives to act in certain ways toward herself and others. In your personal experience with leadership, what have been the

challenges that you have faced and how do they compare to the challenges that Yolanda faces? Describe how some of these challenges made you feel and how you responded to those emotions. What do you see as the areas of success and effectiveness that you have personally experienced that are similar to or different from those experienced by Yolanda?

9. The leadership team of All Our Children strives to work together as an actual team, despite their different points of view. In your personal experience as a leader, how has team building best succeeded? What are the feelings, thought processes, and skills that a leader most needs in order to successfully build teams? How does this apply to a whole team filled with leaders?

10. If you were Yolanda or any of the other leaders of this agency, what would *you* do to understand and solve the problems of this agency? What strengths in yourself, in others, and in the agency workforce would you be aware of and summon up to help you as a leader? What strategies would you develop and use that might be similar to or different from the leaders of All Our Children?

11. If you had "a magic wand" with which to design the funding and a variety of supports to this agency, what would you do? If you had (or could develop) a good relationship with your own representatives in Congress and the state legislature, what would you recommend as the most essential policy changes? Would you include improved compensation (salary and benefits) for the teachers and teaching assistants? How about the leaders—what would you do about their compensation? If these policy changes were enacted and effectively implemented, how would things change? Would they truly make a difference and why?

RESOURCES FOR DELVING DEEPER

Leadership

Bruno, H. E. (2012). *What you need to lead an early childhood program: Emotional intelligence in practice*. Washington, DC: National Association for the Education of Young Children.

Goffin, S. G . (2015). *Professionalizing early childhood education as a field of practice: A guide to the next era*. St. Paul, MN: Redleaf Press.

Goleman, D. (2013). *Focus: The hidden driver of excellence*. New York, NY: Harper.

Goleman, D., Boyatzis , R. E., & McKee, A. (2002). *Primal leadership: Realizing the power of emotional intelligence*. Boston, MA.: Harvard Business School Press.

Nicholson, M. J., & Kroll, L. (2014). Developing leadership for early childhood professionals through oral inquiry: Strengthening equity through making particulars visible in dilemmas of practice. *Early Child Development and Care, 185*, 17–43.

Washington, V ., Gadson, B., & Amel, K.L. (2015). *The new early childhood profes-sional: A step-by-step guide to overcoming Goliath.* New York, NY: Teachers College Press.

Compensation

Bassok, D., Fitzpatrick, M., Loeb, S., & Paglayan, A. (2013). The early childhood care and education workforce from 1990 through 2010: Changing dynamics and persistent concerns. *Education Finance & Policy, 8*(4), 581–601.

National Association for the Education of Young Children (NAEYC). (n.d.). Over-view: power to the profession. Retrieved from www.naeyc.org/profession/over-view

U.S. Department of Health and Human Services & U.S. Department of Education. (2016). *High-quality early learning settings depend on a high-quality work-force: Low compensation undermines quality.* Retrieved from www.acf.hhs. gov/sites/default/files/ecd/ece_low_compensation_undermines_quality_report_june_10_2016_508.pdf

Whitebook, M., Phillips, D., & Howes, C. (2014). *Worthy work, STILL unlivable wages: The early childhood workforce 25 years after the National Child Care Staffing Study.* Berkeley, CA: Center for the Study of Child Care Employment, University of California, Berkeley. Retrieved from cscce.berkeley.edu/files/2014/ReportFINAL.pdf

Family Engagement

Head Start. (2017). Professional development guide: Positive goal-oriented rela-tionships. Retrieved from https://eclkc.ohs.acf.hhs.gov/pdguide/content-areas/engagement-through-positive-goal-oriented-relationships/

Value of Good Teacher Preparation and Ongoing Professional Development

Barnett, W. S., Friedman-Krauss, A. H., Gomez, R. E., Horowitz, M., Weisenfeld, G. G., Clarke Brown, K., & Squires, J. H. (2016). *The state of preschool 2015: State preschool yearbook.* New Brunswick, NJ: National Institute for Early Ed-ucation Research.

Bassok, D. (2013). Raising teacher education levels in Head Start: Exploring pro-grammatic changes between 1999 and 2011. *Early Childhood Research Quar-terly, 28*(4), 83–842. doi:10.1016/j.ecresq.2013.07.004

National Association for the Education of Young Children (NAEYC). (2012). *2010 NAEYC standards for initial & advanced early childhood professional prepa-ration programs.* Washington, DC: NAEYC. Retrieved from www.naeyc.org/caep/files/caep/NAEYC Initial and Advanced Standards 10_2012.pdf

National Association for the Education of Young Children. (2014). *Strategic di-rection.* Retrieved from www.naeyc.org/files/naeyc/NAEYC_Strategic_Direc-tion_2014.pdf

National Head Start Association.. (2015). *Quality Initiative: Head Start perfor-mance excellence and quality recognition program: Quality initiative guidelines and application content.* Retrieved from www.nhsa.org/files/resources/quality_initiative_guidelines_2013-2015.pdf

Value of Social and Emotional Learning

Collaborative for Academic, Social, and Emotional Learning (CASEL). (2017). Core SEL competencies. Retrieved from www.casel.org/core-competencies/

Value of Early Math

Brenneman, K., Boller, K., Atkins-Burnett, S., Stipek, D., Forry, N., Ertle, B., . . . Schultz, T, (2011). Measuring the quality of early childhood math and science curricula and teaching. In M. Zaslow, L. Martinez-Beck, K. Tout, & T. Halle (Eds.), *Quality Measurement in Early Childhood Settings* (pp. 77–103). Baltimore, MD: Paul H. Brookes.

Schoenfeld, A., & Stipek, D. (2011). *Math matters: Children's mathematical journeys start early.* Report of a conference held November 7 & 8. Berkeley, CA., Retrieved from earlymath.org

Stipek, D. J., & Valentino, R. A. (2015). Early childhood memory and attention as predictors of academic growth trajectories. *Journal of Educational Psychology, 107*(3), 771–788. doi:10.1037/edu0000004

Value of Early Literacy

Boyce, L., & Snow, C. E. (2009). Diverse paths to literacy: Family factors and program effects among preschool-aged children [Special Issue]. *Scientific Studies of Reading, 13*(2).

Resnick, L. B., Snow, C. E., & New Standards (Organization). Speaking and Listening Committee. (2009). *Speaking and listening for preschool through third grade* (Rev. ed.). Newark, DE: New Standards/International Reading Association.

Snow, C. E. (2015). Fifty years of research on reading. In M. J. Feuer, A. Berman, & R. Atkinson (Eds.), *Past as prologue: The National Academy of Education at 50: Members reflect* (pp. 175–180). Washington, DC: National Academy of Education.

Value of Adult Speech to Infants

Weisleder, A., & Fernald, A. (2013). Talking to children matters: early language experience strengthens processing and builds vocabulary. *Psychological Science, 24*(11), 2143–2152. doi:10.1177/0956797613488145

Using Data to Improve Outcomes

Center for the Study of Child Care Employment. (n.d.). About Us. Retrieved from http://cscce.berkeley.edu/about/

Derrick-Mills, T., Sandstrom, H., Pettijohn, S., Fyffe, S., & Koulish, J. (2014). *Data use for continuous quality improvement: What the Head Start field can learn from other disciplines: A literature review and conceptual framework* (OPRE Report # 2014-77). Washington, DC: Office of Planning, Research and Evaluation, Administration for Children and Families. U.S. Department of Health and Human Services.

Conclusion

A deep love for young children and a firm conviction that all of us should join together to give them the best possible start in life drew me to the decision to research and write this book.

Other than the decision to focus the book ultimately around the promotion of emotional and social intelligence in children and the adults who are important to them in their preschool settings—and the decision to accomplish this goal by developing teaching cases that can be used to educate early childhood teachers and leaders—I allowed the rest of the book to evolve.

Three endeavors influenced its evolution:

1. Reviews of early childhood research so I could identify the elements of emotional and social intelligence that I might look for in classroom and leadership-meeting observations
2. Many strength-based classroom and leadership-meeting observations in which I identified challenging scenarios that teachers and leaders were responding to with great skill
3. In-depth interviews with teachers and leaders who permitted me to enter their inner worlds and discover why they employed their skills—what philosophies and beliefs infused their skills

I've felt a strong sense of connection all along this "evolutionary path" to the many devoted human beings who work long hours for much less pay than they can earn elsewhere in order to help young children and their families get the best possible start in life. May we, as a nation, celebrate and honor those glorious individuals. May we continue to offer them those professional opportunities for improving their skills and knowledge that are excellent—and may we improve the opportunities that are less than excellent.

Finally, may we respond to all their devotion with an equal devotion to ensuring that they have a worthy wage, one that allows them to stay in the field that they love, working with the children and families they love.

I hope this book will be very useful to our field, and I welcome any feedback the reader might want to offer.

Recommended Reading

Aber, J. L., Jones, S. M., & Raver, C. C. (2007). Poverty and child development: New perspectives on a defining issue. In J. L. Aber, S. J. Bishop-Josef, S. M. Jones, K. T. McLearn, & D. A. Phillips (Eds.), *Child development and social policy: Knowledge for action* (1st ed., pp. 149–166). Washington, DC: American Psychological Association.

Agostin, T. M., & Bain, S. K. (1997). Predicting early school success with developmental and social skills screeners. *Psychology in the Schools, 34*(3), 219–228. doi:10.1002/(SICI)1520-6807(199707)34:3<219::AID-PITS4>3.0.CO;2-J

Aikens, N. L., Coleman, C. P., & Barbarin, O. A. (2007). Ethnic differences in the effects of parental depression on preschool children's socioemotional functioning. *Social Development, 17*(1), 137–160. doi:10.1111/j.1467-9507.2007.00420.x

Baker, A. C., Manfredi-Petitt, L. A., & National Association for the Education of Young Children. (2004). *Relationships, the heart of quality care: Creating community among adults in early care settings*. Washington, DC: National Association for the Education of Young Children.

Bar-On, R. (2006). The Bar-On model of emotional-social intelligence (ESI). *Psicothema, 18*(supl.), 13–25.

Barbarin, O. A. (2002). Culture and ethnicity in social, emotional and academic development. In Ewing Marion Kauffman Foundation (Ed.), *Set for success: Building a strong foundation for school readiness based on the social–emotional development of young children* (Vol. 1, pp. 45–65). Kansas City, MO: The Kauffman Early Education Exchange.

Barbarin, O. A. (2006). ABLE: A system for mental health screening and care for preschool children. In B. T. Bowman & E. Moore (Eds.), *School readiness and social–emotional development: Perspectives on cultural diversity* (pp. 76–88). Washington, DC: National Black Child Development Institute.

Barbarin, O. A., Bryant, D., McCandies, T. T., Burchinal, M., Early, D., Clifford, R. M., . . . Howes, C. (2006). Children enrolled in public pre-K: The relation of family life, neighborhood quality, and socioeconomic resources to early competence. *American Journal of Orthopsychiatry, 76*(2), 265–276. doi:10.1037/0002-9432.76.2.265

Barbarin, O. A., McCandies, T. T., Early, D., Clifford, R. M., Bryant, D., Burchinal, M., . . . Pianta, R. C. (2006). Quality of prekindergarten: What families are looking for in public sponsored programs. *Early Education and Development, 17*(4), 619–642. doi:10.1207/s15566935eed1704_6

Barnard, K. E., Bigsby, R., Field, T., Greenspan, S. L., Heimann, M., Hofer, M., . . . Zimmerman, L. (2010). *Nurturing children and families: Building on the legacy of T. Berry Brazelton*. Malden, MA: Wiley-Blackwell.

Barnes, L. B., Christensen, C. R., and Hansen, A. J. (1994). *Teaching and the case method: Text, cases, and readings* (3rd ed.). Boston, MA: Harvard Business School Press.

Bay Area Network for Diversity Training in Early Childhood. (2003). *Reaching for answers: A workbook on diversity in early childhood education.* Oakland, CA: Bandtec.

Bayat, M., Mindes, G., & Covitt, S. (2010). What does RTI (response to intervention) look like in preschool? *Early Childhood Education Journal, 37,* 493–500.

Belenky, M. F. (1986). *Women's ways of knowing: The development of self, voice, and mind.* New York, NY: Basic Books.

Belenky, M. F., Bond, L. A., & Weinstock, J. S. (1997). *A tradition that has no name: Nurturing the development of people, families, and communities.* New York, NY: Basic Books.

Berk, L. E., & Winsler, A. (1995). *Scaffolding children's learning: Vygotsky and early childhood education* (Vol. 7). Washington, DC: National Association for the Education of Young Children.

Biddle, J. K. (2012). *The three rs of leadership: Building effective early childhood programs through relationships, reciprocal learning, and reflection.* Washington, DC: National Association for the Education of Young Children.

Bierman, K. L., Domitrovich, C. E., Nix, R. L., Gest, S. D., Welsh, J. A., Greenberg, M. T., . . . Gill, S. (2008). Promoting academic and social–emotional school readiness: The Head Start REDI program. *Child Development, 79*(6), 1802–1817. doi:10.1111/j.1467-8624.2008.01227.x

Bierman, K. L., Nix, R. L., & Greenberg, M. T. (2008). Executive functions and school readiness intervention: impact, moderation, and mediation in the Head Start REDI program. *Development and Psychopathology, 20*(3), 821–843. doi:10.1017/S0954579408000394

Birch, S. H., & Ladd, G. W. (1997). The teacher–child relationship and children's early school adjustment. *Journal of School Psychology, 35*(1), 61–79. doi:0022-4405/97

Blair, C. (2003). Self-regulation and school readiness. *ERIC Digest* (ED477640). Retrieved from www.eric.ed.gov/ERICWebPortal/Home.portal?_nf-pb=true&ERICExtSearch_SearchValue_0=ED477640&ERICExt-Search_SearchType_0=no&_pageLabel=ERICSearchResult&new-Search=true&rnd=1169450487712&searchtype=basic

Blair, C., & Diamond, A. (2008). Biological processes in prevention and intervention: The promotion of self-regulation as a means of preventing school failure. *Development and Psychopathology, 20*(3), 899–911. doi:10.1017/S0954579408000436

Blair, C., Knipe, H., Cummings, E., Baker, D. P., Gamson, D., Eslinger, P., & Thorne, S. L. (2007). A developmental neuroscience approach to the study of school readiness. In R. C. Pianta, M. J. Cox, & K. L. Snow (Eds.), *School readiness and the transition to kindergarten in the era of accountability* (pp. 149–174). Baltimore, MD: Paul H. Brookes.

Blair, C., Zelazo, P. D., & Greenberg, M. T. (2005). The measurement of executive function in early childhood. *Developmental Neuropsychology, 28*(2), 561–571. doi:10.1207/s15326942dn2802_1

Boutte, G. S., & DeFlorimonte, D. (1998). The complexities of valuing cultural differences without overemphasizing them: Taking it to the next level. *Equity and Excellence in Education, 31*(3), 54–62. doi:10.1080/1066568980310308

Bowlby, J. (1982). *Attachment* (2nd ed., Vol. 1). New York, NY: Basic Books.

Bowman, B. (2006). Resilience: Preparing children for school. In B. Bowman & E. K. Moore (Eds.), *School readiness and social–emotional development: Perspectives on cultural diversity* (pp. 49–57). Washington, DC: National Black Child Development Institute.

Bowman, B. T. (2006). School readiness and social–emotional development. In B. T. Bowman & E. Moore (Eds.), *School readiness and social–emotional development: perspectives on cultural diversity* (pp. 33–47). Washington, DC: National Black Child Development Institute.

Bowman, B. T., Donovan, M. S., & Burns, M. S. (Eds.). (2001). *Eager to learn: Educating our preschoolers.* Washington, DC: The National Academies Press.

Bowman, B. T., & Moore, E. (Eds.). (2006). *School readiness and social–emotional development: perspectives on cultural diversity.* Washington, DC: National Black Child Development Institute.

Boyd, J., Barnett, W. S., Bodrova, E., Leong, D. J., Gomby, D., Robin, K. B., & Hustedt, J. T. (2005). *Promoting children's social and emotional development through preschool* (NIEER Policy Report). New Brunswick, NJ: National Institute for Early Education Research. Retrieved from nieer.org/policy-issue/policy-report-promoting-childrens-social-and-emotional-development-through-preschool-education

Brackett, M. A., & Katulak, N. A. (2006). Emotional intelligence in the classroom: Skill-based training for teachers and students. In J. Ciarrochi & J. D. Mayer (Ed.), *Improving emotional intelligence: A practitioner's guide.* New York, NY: Psychology Press.

Brackett, M. A., & Kremenitzer, J. P. (Eds.). (in press). *Emotional literacy in the elementary school: Six steps to promote social competence and academic performance.* Port Chester, NY: National Professional Resources.

Brackett, M. A., Kremenitzer, J. P., Mauer, M., Carpenter, M. D., Rivers, S. E., & Katulak, N. A. (Eds.). (2007). *Emotional literacy in the classroom: Upper elementary.* Port Chester, NY: National Professional Resources.

Brackett, M. A., Mayer, J. D., & Warner, R. M. (2004). Emotional intelligence and its relation to everyday behaviour. *Personality and Individual Differences, 36*(6), 1387–1402. doi:http://dx.doi.org/10.1016/S0191-8869(03)00236-8

Brazelton, T. B., & Sparrow, J. D. (2006). *Touchpoints—birth to three: Your child's emotional and behavioral development* (2nd ed.). Cambridge, MA: Da Capo Press.

Bronson, M. (2000). *Self-regulation in early childhood: Nature and nurture.* New York, NY: Guilford Press.

Brooks-Gunn, J., Rouse, C. E., & McLanahan, S. (2007). Racial and ethnic gaps in school readiness. In R. C. Pianta, M. J. Cox, & K. L. Snow (Eds.), *School readiness and the transition to kindergarten in the era of accountability* (pp. 283–306). Baltimore, MD: Paul H. Brookes.

Brownell, C. A., & Kopp, C. B. (2007). *Socioemotional development in the toddler years: Transitions and transformations.* New York, NY: Guilford Press.

Bruno, H. E. (2012). *What you need to lead an early childhood program: Emotional intelligence in practice*. Washington, DC: National Association for the Education of Young Children.

Bulotsky-Shearer, R. J., & Fantuzzo, J. W. (2011). Preschool behavior problems in classroom learning situations and literacy outcomes in kindergarten and first grade. *Early Childhood Research Quarterly, 26*(1), 61–73.

Burchinal, M., Peisner-Feinberg, E., Pianta, R. C., & Howes, C. (2002). Development of academic skills from preschool through second grade: Family and classroom predictors of developmental trajectories. *Journal of School Psychology, 40*(5), 415–436.

California Department of Education. (2000). *Prekindergarten learning and development guidelines*. Sacramento: California Department of Education.

California Department of Education & First 5 California (Eds.). (2011). *California early childhood educator competencies*. Sacramento: California Department of Education.

California Department of Education, Child Development Division. (2013). *California Preschool Curriculum Framework* (Vol. 3). Sacramento: California Department of Education.

California Department of Education, Child Development Division. (2012). *California preschool learning foundations* (Vol. 3). Sacramento: California Department of Education.

Center on the Developing Child at Harvard University. (2007). *A science-based framework for early childhood policy: Using evidence to improve outcomes in learning, behavior, and health for vulnerable children.* Retrieved from developingchild.harvard.edu/wp-content/uploads/2015/05/Policy_Framework.pdf

Center on the Social and Emotional Foundations for Early Learning. (n.d.). Center on the Social and Emotional Foundations for Early Learning. Retrieved from csefel.vanderbilt.edu

Center on the Social and Emotional Foundations for Early Learning. (2006). *Facilitator's guide: Promoting the social emotional competence of young children.* Urbana: University of Illinois at Urbana-Champaign, The Center on the Social and Emotional Foundations for Early Learning. Retrieved from csefel.vanderbilt.edu/modules/facilitators-guide.pdf

Chentsova-Dutton, Y. E., Chu, J. P. C., Tsai, J. L., Rottenberg, J., Gross, J. J., & Gotlib, I. H. (2007). Depression and emotional reactivity: Variation among Asian Americans of East Asian descent and European Americans. *Journal of Abnormal Psychology, 116*(4), 776–785.

Chentsova-Dutton, Y. E., & Tsai, J. L. (2007). Gender differences in emotional response among European Americans and Hmong Americans. *Cognition and Emotion, 21*(1), 162–181.

Cohen, D. H., Stern, V., Balaban, N., & Gropper, N. (2008). *Observing and recording the behavior of young children* (5th ed.). New York, NY: Teachers College Press.

Cohen, J. A., Onunaku, N., Clothier, S., & Pope, J. (2005). *Helping young children succeed: Strategies to promote early childhood social and emotional development.* Retrieved from www.zerotothree.org/resources/136-helping-young-children-succeed-strategies-to-promote-early-childhood-social-and-emotional-development

College of Health & Human Development Prevention Research Center. (2006). Harrisburg Preschool Program (HPP). Retrieved from www.prevention.psu. edu/completed-projects-prevention-research-center

Conduct Problems Prevention Research Group. (1999). Initial impact of the fast track prevention trial for conduct problems: II. Classroom effects. *Journal of Consulting and Clinical Psychology, 67*(5), 648–657.

Daniel, J. (2009). Intentionally thoughtful family engagement in early childhood education. *Young Children, 64*(5), 10–14.

Domitrovich, C. E., Cortes, R. C., & Greenberg, M. T. (2007). Improving young children's social and emotional competence: A randomized trial of the pre-school "PATHS" curriculum. *The Journal of Primary Prevention, 28*(2), 67–91.

Domitrovich, C. E., Gest, S. D., Gill, S., Bierman, K. L., Welsh, J. A., & Jones, D. (2009). Fostering high-quality teaching with an enriched cur-riculum and professional development support: The Head Start REDI program. *American Educational Research Journal, 46*(2), 567–597. doi:10.3102/0002831208328089

Doucet, F., & Tudge, J. (2007). Co-constructing the transition to school: Reframing the novice versus expert roles of children, parents, and teachers from a cultural perspective. In R. C. Pianta, M. J. Cox, & K. L. Snow (Eds.), *School readiness and the transition to kindergarten in the era of accountability* (pp. 307–328). Baltimore, MD: Paul H. Brookes.

Downer, J. (2007). Father involvement during early childhood. In R. C. Pianta, M. J. Cox, & K. L. Snow (Eds.), *School readiness and the transition to kindergarten in the era of accountability* (pp. 329–354). Baltimore, MD: Paul H. Brookes.

Duncan, G. J., Dowsett, C. J., Claessens, A., Magnuson, K., Huston, A. C., Kleban-ov, P., . . . Japel, C. (2007). School readiness and later achievement. *Develop-mental Psychology, 43*(6), 1428–1446.

Durlak, J. A., & Weissberg, R. P. (2005). *A major meta-analysis of positive youth development programs.* Paper presented at the American Psychological Associ-ation Annual Convention, Washington, DC.

Durlak, J. A., & Weissberg, R. P. (2007). *The impact of after-school programs that promote personal and social skills.* Chicago, IL: Collaborative for Academic, Social, and Emotional Learning.

Eisenberg, N., Ma, Y., Chang, L., Zhou, Q., Aiken, L., & West, S. (2007). Relations of effortful control, reactive undercontrol, and anger to Chinese children's ad-justment. *Development and Psychopathology, 19*, 385–409.

Eisenberg, N., Valiente, C., & Eggum, N. (2010). Self-regulation and school readi-ness. *Early Education and Development, 21*(5), 681–698.

Eisenberg, N., Zhou, Q., Spinrad, T. L., Valiente, C., Fabes, R. A., & Liew, J. C. (2005). Relations among positive parenting, children's effortful control, and externalizing problems: A three-wave longitudinal study. *Child Development, 76*(5), 1055–1071.

Elias, M. J., Tobias, S. E., & Friedlander, B. S. (1999). *Emotionally intelligent par-enting: How to raise a self-disciplined, responsible, socially skilled child.* New York, NY: Three Rivers Press.

Elkind, D. (2007). *The power of play: How spontaneous, imaginative activities lead to happier, healthier children.* Cambridge, MA: Da Capo Press.

Erikson, E. H. (1950). *Childhood and society.* New York, NY: Norton.

Espinosa, L. M. (1995). Hispanic parent involvement in early childhood programs. ERIC Digest (ED382412). Retrieved from www.ericdigests.org/1996-1/hispanic.htm doi:ED382412

Espinosa, L. M. (2002). *High-quality preschool: Why we need it and what it looks like* (NIEER Policy Brief, Issue 1). Preschool Policy Matters. New Brunswick, NJ: National Institute for Early Education Research. Retrieved from nieer.org/policy-issue/policy-brief-high-quality-preschool-why-we-need-it-and-what-it-looks-like

Espinosa, L. M. (2002). The connections between social–emotional development and early literacy. In *Set for success: Building a strong foundation for school readiness based on the social-emotional development of young children* (pp. 30–44). The Kauffman Early Education Exchange (Vol. 1, no. 1). Kansas City, MO: The Ewing Marion Kauffman Foundation. Retrieved from www.research-connections.org/childcare/resources/2421

Espinosa, L. M. (2006). Social, cultural, and linguistic features of school readiness in young Latino children. In B. Bowman & E. K. Moore (Eds.), *School readiness and social–emotional development: Perspectives on cultural diversity* (pp. 33–47). Washington, DC: National Black Child Development Institute.

Ewing Marion Kauffman Foundation. (2002). *Set for Success: Building a Strong Foundation for School Readiness Based on the Social–emotional Development of Young Children*. The Kauffman Early Education Exchange. (Vol. 1, no. 1). Kansas City, MO: Ewing Marion Kauffman Foundation.

Fabes, R. A., Gaertner, B. M., Popp, T. K. (2006). Getting along with others: Social competence in early childhood. In K. M. D. Phillips (Ed.), *Blackwell handbook of early childhood development* (pp. 297–316). Malden, MA: Blackwell.

Fantuzzo, J. W., Bulotsky-Shearer, R. J., Fusco, R. A., & McWayne, C. (2005). An investigation of preschool classroom behavioral adjustment problems and social–emotional school readiness competencies. *Early Childhood Research Quarterly, 20*(3), 259–275.

Florez, I. R. (2011). Case-based instruction in early childhood teacher preparation: Does it work? *Journal of Childhood Teacher Education, 32*(2), 118–134.

Fraiberg, S. (2008). *The magic years: Understanding and handling the problems of early childhood.* New York, NY: Scribner.

Fredericks, L., Weissberg, R., Resnik, H., Patrikakou, E., & O'Brien, M. U. (2004). *Schools, families, and social and emotional learning: Ideas and tools for working with parents and families.* Chicago, IL: Collaborative for Academic, Social, and Emotional Learning. Retrieved from eric.ed.gov/?id=ED505371

Fuller, B. (with Bridges, M., & Pai, S.). (2007). *Standardized childhood: The political and cultural struggle over early education.* Stanford, CA: Stanford University Press.

Fung, H. (2006). Affect and early moral socialization: Some insights and contributions from indigenous psychological studies in Taiwan. In U. Kim, K.-S. Yang, & K.-K. Hwang (Eds.), *Indigenous and cultural psychology: Understanding people in context* (pp. 175–197). New York, NY: Springer.

Fung, H., & Smith, B. (2009). Learning morality. In D. F. Lancy, J. Bock, & S. Gaskins (Eds.), *The anthropology of learning in childhood* (pp. 261–285). Lanham, MD: Rowman & Littlefield.

Garcia, E. E., & Cuellar, D. (2006). Who are these linguistically and culturally diverse students? *Teachers College Record, 108*(11), 2220–2246.

García, E. E., & Jensen, B. (2007). Helping young Hispanic learners. *Educational Leadership, 64*(6), 34–39.

García, E. E., & Miller, L. S. (2007). An introduction to this special thematic issue. *Journal of Latinos and Education, 6*(3), 205–208.

Gardner, H. (2006). *Multiple intelligences: New horizons* (Completely rev. and updated ed.). New York, NY: Basic Books.

Gazelle, H., & Ladd, G. W. (2003). Anxious solitude and peer exclusion: A diathesis-stress model of internalizing trajectories in childhood. *Child Development, 74*(1), 257–278.

Goleman, D. (2000). An EI-based theory of performance. In C. Cherniss & D. Goleman (Eds.), *The emotionally intelligent workplace.* San Francisco, CA: Jossey-Bass.

Goleman, D. (2003). *Healing emotions: Conversations with the Dalai Lama on mindfulness, emotions, and health.* Boston, MA: Shambhala.

Goleman, D. (2006). *Social intelligence: The new science of human relationships.* New York, NY: Bantam Books.

Gormley, W. T. J., Phillips, D. A., Newmark, K., Welti, K., & Adelstein, S. (2011). Social–emotional effects of early childhood education programs in Tulsa. *Child Development, 82*(6), 2095–2109.

Gottman, J. M., Katz, L. F., & Hooven, C. (1997). *Meta-emotion: How families communicate emotionally.* Mahwah, NJ: Lawrence Erlbaum Associates.

Gottman, J. M., & DeClaire, J. (1997). *The heart of parenting: How to raise an emotionally intelligent child.* New York, NY: Simon & Schuster.

Greenberg, M. T., Blair, C., & Zelazo, P. D. (2005). The measurement of executive function in early childhood. *Developmental Neuropsychology, 28*(2), 561–171.

Greenberg, M. T., Kusche, C. A., Cook, E. T., & Quamma, J. P. (1995). Promoting emotional competence in school-aged children: The effects of the PATHS curriculum. *Development and Psychopathology, 7,* 117–136.

Hammer, C. S., Lawrence, F. R., & Miccio, A. W. (2008). Exposure to English before and after entry into Head Start: Bilingual children's receptive language growth in Spanish and English. *International Journal of Bilingual Education and Bilingualism, 11*(1), 30–56. doi:10.2167/beb376.0

Hammer, C. S., & Miccio, A. (2006). Early language and reading development of bilingual preschoolers from low-income families. *Topics in Language Disorders, 26*(4), 322–337.

Hammer, C. S., Rodriguez, B. L., Lawrence, F. R., & Miccio, A. W. (2007). Puerto Rican mothers' beliefs and home literacy practices. *Language, Speech, and Hearing Services in Schools, 38,* 216–224. doi:10.1044/0161-1461(2007/023)

Hannaford, C. (1995). *Smart moves: Why learning is not all in your head.* Arlington, VA: Great Ocean Publishers.

Harme, B. K., & Pianta, R. C. (2007). Learning opportunities in preschool and early Elementary classrooms. In R. C. Pianta, M. J. Cox, & K. L. Snow (Eds.), *School readiness and the transition to kindergarten in the era of accountability* (pp. 49–84). Baltimore, MD: Paul H. Brookes.

Hemmeter, M. L., Ostrosky, M. M., Artman, K. M., & Kinder, K. A. (2008). Moving right along . . . Planning transitions to prevent challenging behavior. *Young Children, 63*(3), 18–25.

Hernandez, D. J., Denton, N. A., & Macartney, S. E. (2007). Demographic trends and the transition years. In R. C. Pianta, M. J. Cox, & K. L. Snow (Eds.), *School readiness and the transition to kindergarten in the era of accountability* (pp. 217–282). Baltimore, MD: Paul H. Brookes.

Hirschland, D. (2008). *Collaborative intervention in early childhood: Consulting with parents and teachers of 3- to 7-year-olds.* New York, NY: Oxford University Press.

Howes, C. (2000). Social–emotional classroom climate in child care, child–teacher relationships,and children's second grade peer relations. *Social Development,* 9(2), 191–204.

Howes, C., Burchinal, M., Pianta, R., Bryant, D., Early, D., Clifford, R., & Barbarin, O. A. (2008). Ready to learn? Children's pre-academic achievement in pre-kindergarten programs. *Early Childhood Research Quarterly, 23,* 27–50.

Izard, C. E. (1977). *Human emotions.* New York, NY: Plenum Press.

Izard, C. E., Trentacosta, C. J., King, K. A., & Mostow, A. J. (2004). An emotion-based prevention program for Head Start children. *Early Education and Development, 15*(4), 407–422.

Jackson, S. E., Schwab, R. L., & Schuler, R. S. (1986). Toward an understanding of the burnout phenomenon. *Journal of Applied Psychology, 71*(4), 630–640.

Johnson, K., & Knitzer, J. (2006). *Early childhood comprehensive systems that spend smarter: Maximizing resources to serve vulnerable young children.* New York, NY: National Center for Children in Poverty. Retrieved from nccp.org/publications/pdf/text_655.pdf

Joseph, G. E., & Strain, P. S. (2006). *Enhancing emotional vocabulary in young children. Handout 2.6: Social Emotional Teaching Strategies.* [Nashville, TN]: Vanderbilt University, Center on the Social and Emotional Foundations for Early Learning. Retrieved from csefel.vanderbilt.edu/modules/module2/handout6.pdf

Joseph, G. E., Strain, P. S., & Ostrosky, M. M. (2005). *Fostering emotional literacy in young children: Labeling emotions.* [Nashville, TN]: Vanderbilt University, Center on the Social and Emotional Foundations for Early Learning. Retrieved from csefel.vanderbilt.edu/kits/wwbtk21.pdf

Kagan, S. L., & Kauerz, K. (2007). Reaching for the whole: Integration and alignment in early education policy. In R. C. Pianta, M. J. Cox, & K. L. Snow (Eds.), *School readiness and the transition to kindergarten in the era of accountability* (pp. 11–30). Baltimore, MD: Paul H. Brookes.

Kam, C.-M., Greenberg, M. T., & Gusche, C. A. (2004). Sustained effects of the PATHS curriculum on the social and psychological adjustment of children in special education. *Journal of Emotional and Behavioral Disorders, 12*(2), 66–78.

Kegan, R. (1982). *The evolving self: Problem and process in human development.* Cambridge, MA: Harvard University Press.

Kegan, R. (1994). *In over our heads: The mental demands of modern life.* Cambridge, MA: Harvard University Press.

Knitzer, J. (2000). *Promoting resilience: Helping young children and parents affected by substance abuse, domestic violence, and depression in the context of welfare reform.* New York, NY: National Center for Children in Poverty. Retrieved from nccp.org/publications/pdf/text_389.pdf

Knitzer, J. (2002). *Promoting the emotional well-being of children and families.* New York, NY: National Center for Children in Poverty. Retrieved from www.nccp.org/publications/pdf/text_485.pdf

Knitzer, J. (2004). The challenge of mental health in Head Start: Making the vision real. In E. F. Zigler & S. Styfco (Eds.), *The Head Start debates* (pp. 179–192). Baltimore, MD: Paul H. Brookes.

Kopp, C. B. (2003). *Baby steps: A guide to your child's social, physical, mental, and emotional development in the first two years* (2nd ed.). New York, NY: Henry Holt.

Kremenitzer, J. P. (2005). The emotionally intelligent early childhood educator: Self-reflective journaling. *Early Childhood Education Journal, 33*(1), 3–9.

Kremenitzer, J. P., & Miller, R. (2008). Are you a highly qualified, emotionally intelligent early childhood educator? *Young Children, 63*(4), 106–112.

Ladd, G. W., & Burgess, K. B. (1999). Charting the relationship trajectories of aggressive, withdrawn, and aggressive/withdrawn children during early grade school. *Child Development, 70*(4), 910–929.

Ladd, G. W., Kochenderfer, B. J., & Coleman, C. C. (1997). Classroom peer acceptance, friendship, and victimization: Distinct relational systems that contribute uniquely to children's school adjustment? *Child Development, 68*(6), 1181–1197. doi:10.2307/1132300

Lester, B. M., & Sparrow, J. D. (Eds.). (2010). *Nurturing children and families: Building on the legacy of T. Berry Brazelton.* Oxford, United Kingdom: Wiley-Blackwell.

Levin, D. E., & Carlsson-Paige, N. (2006). *The war play dilemma: What every parent and teacher needs to know* (2nd ed.). New York, NY: Teachers College Press.

Lewin-Benham, A. W. (2006). *Possible schools: The Reggio approach to urban education.* New York, NY: Teachers College Press.

LoCasale-Crouch, J., Konold, T., Pianta, R. C., Howes, C., Burchinal, M., Bryant, D., . . . Barbarin, O. A. (2007). Observed classroom quality profiles in state-funded pre-kindergarten programs and associations with teacher, program, and classroom characteristics. *Early Childhood Research Quarterly, 22*, 3–17.

Mashburn, A. J., Pianta, R. C., Hamre, B. K., Downer, J. T., Barbarin, O. A., Bryant, D., . . . Howes, C. (2008). Measures of classroom quality in prekindergarten and children's development of academic, language, and social skills. *Child Development, 79*(3), 732–749. doi:10.1111/j.1467-8624.2008.01154.x

McCabe, L. A., & Frede, E. C. (2007). *Challenging behaviors and the role of preschool education* (NIEER Policy Brief, Issue 16). New Brunswick, NJ: National Institute for Early Education Research.

McClelland, M. M., Morrison, F. J., & Holmes, D. L. (2000). Children at risk for early academic problems: The role of learning-related social skills. *Early Childhood Research Quarterly, 15*(3), 307–329.

Meisels, S. J. (2007). No easy answers: accountability in early childhood. In R. C. Pianta, M. J. Cox, & K. L. Snow (Eds.), *School readiness and the transition to kindergarten in the era of accountability* (pp. 31–48). Baltimore, MD: Paul H. Brookes.

Mendez, J. A., McDermott, P., & Fantuzzo, J. (2002). Identifying and promoting social competence with African American preschool children: Developmental and contextual considerations. *Psychology in the Schools, 39*(1), 111–123.

Mesa-Bains, A., & Shulman, J. H. (Eds.). (1994). *Facilitator's guide to diversity in the classroom*. Hillsdale, New Jersey: Lawrence Erlbaum Associates.

Miccio, A. W., Tabors, P. O., Páez, M. M., Hammer, C. S., & Wagstaff, D. A. (2005). Vocabulary development in Spanish-speaking Head Start children of Puerto Rican descent. In J. Cohen, K. T. McAlister, K. Rolstad, & J. MacSwan (Eds.), *Proceedings of the 4th International Symposium on Bilingualism* (pp. 1614–1617). Somerville, MA: Cascadilla Press.

Miller, P. J., Fung, H., & Koven, M. (2007). Narrative reverberations: How participation in narrative practices co-creates persons and cultures. In S. Kitayama & D. Cohen (Eds.), *Handbook of cultural psychology* (pp. 595–614). New York, NY: Guilford Press.

Mindess, M., Chen, M.-h., & Brenner, R. (2008, November). Social–emotional learning in the primary curriculum. *Beyond the Journal: Young Children on the Web, 56*–60.

Moore, E. K. (2006). The NBCDI social–emotional development project. In B. T. Bowman & E. K. Moore (Eds.), *School readiness and social–emotional development: Perspectives on cultural diversity*. Washington, DC: National Black Child Development Institute.

Nathanson, L., Rivers, S. E., Flynn, L. M., & Brackett, M. A. (2016). Creating emotionally intelligent schools with RULER. *Emotion Review, 8*(4), 305–310. doi:10.1177/1754073916650495

National Association for the Education of Young Children. (2011). Critical facts about the early childhood workforce. Retrieved from www.naeyc.org/policy/advocacy/ECWorkforceFacts

National Forum on Early Childhood Program Evaluation. (2007). *Early childhood program evaluations: A decision-maker's guide*. Retrieved from developingchild.harvard.edu/resources/early-childhood-program-evaluations-a-decision-makers-guide /

National Research Council. (2000). *How People Learn: Brain, Mind, Experience, and School: Expanded Edition*. Washington, DC: The National Academies Press. https://doi.org/10.17226/9853.

National Scientific Council on the Developing Child. (2004a). *Children's emotional development is built into the architecture of their brains (Working Paper No. 2)*. Retrieved from developingchild.harvard.edu/resources/childrens-emotional-development-is-built-into-the-architecture-of-their-brains/

National Scientific Council on the Developing Child. (2004b). *Young children develop in an environment of relationships (Working Paper No. 1)*. Retrieved from developingchild.harvard.edu/resources/wp1/

National Scientific Council on the Developing Child. (2005/2014). *Excessive stress disrupts the architecture of the developing brain (Working Paper 3)*. Retrieved from developingchild.harvard.edu/resources/wp3/

National Scientific Council on the Developing Child. (2007). The science of early childhood development: Closing the gap between what we know and what we do. Retrieved from developingchild.harvard.edu/index.php/resources/reports_and_working_papers/science_of_early_childhood_development/

National Scientific Council on the Developing Child. (2008/2012). *Establishing a level foundation for life: Mental health begins in early childhood (Working Paper No. 6)*. Retrieved from developingchild.harvard.edu/resources/establishing-a-level-foundation-for-life-mental-health-begins-in-early-childhood/

National Scientific Council on the Developing Child. (2010). *Early experiences can alter gene expression and affect long-term development (Working Paper No. 10)*. Retrieved from developingchild.harvard.edu/resources/early-experiences-can-alter-gene-expression-and-affect-long-term-development/

National Scientific Council on the Developing Child. (2011). Building the brain's "air traffic control" system: How early experiences shape the development of executive function (Working Paper No. 11). Retrieved from developingchild.harvard.edu/resources/building-the-brains-air-traffic-control-system-how-early-experiences-shape-the-development-of-executive-function/

Nelson, G., Westhues, A., & MacLeod, J. (2003). A meta-analysis of longitudinal research on preschool prevention programs for children. *Prevention and Treatment, 6* (Article 31).

Nemeth, K. N., & National Association for the Education of Young Children. (2012). *Basics of supporting dual language learners: An introduction for educators of children from birth through age 8*. Washington, DC: National Association for the Education of Young Children.

Norton, D. G. (2006). Research methods and issues for the study of African American children and school achievement. In B. Bowman & E. K. Moore (Eds.), *School readiness and social–emotional development: Perspectives on cultural diversity* (pp. 58–75). Washington, DC: National Black Child Development Institute.

Obradovi, J., Portilla, X. A., & Boyce, T. W. (2012). Executive functioning and developmental neuroscience. In R. C. Piata, L. Justice, W. S. Barnett, & S. Sheridan (Eds.), *Handbook of early childhood education* (pp. 324–351). New York, NY: Guilford Press.

Palmer, P. J. (2004). *A hidden wholeness: The journey toward an undivided life*. San Francisco, CA: Jossey-Bass.

Palmer, P. J. (2007). *The courage to teach: Exploring the inner landscape of a teacher's life* (10th anniversary ed.). San Francisco, CA: Jossey-Bass.

Parker, J. G., & Gottman, J. M. (1989). Social and emotional development in a relational context. In T. J. Berndt & G. W. Ladd (Eds.), *Peer relationships in child development*. New York, NY: John Wiley & Sons.

Pascoe, J. M., Shaikh, U., Forbis, S. G., & Etzel, R. A. (2007). Health and nutrition as a foundation for success in school. In R. C. Pianta, M. J. Cox, & K. L. Snow (Eds.), *School readiness and the transition to kindergarten in the era of accountability* (pp. 99–120). Baltimore, MD: Paul H. Brookes.

PATHS® Education Worldwide (n.d.). What is the *PATHS*® curriculum? Retrieved from www.pathseducation.com/what-is-paths/paths-curriculum

Pianta, R. C., Cox, M. J., & Snow, K. L. (Eds.). (2007). *School readiness and the transition to kindergarten in the era of accountability*. Baltimore, MD: Paul H. Brookes.

Pianta, R. C., & Howes, C. (Eds.). (2009). *The promise of pre-K*. Baltimore, MD: Brookes Publishing.

Posner, M. I., & Rothbart, M. K. (2000). Developing mechanisms of self-regulation. *Development and Psychopathology, 12,* 427–441.

Raikes, H. A., & Thompson, R. A. (2005). Links between risk and attachment security: Models of influence. *Applied Developmental Psychology, 26,* 440–455.

Raikes, H. A., & Thompson, R. A. (2006). Family emotional climate, attachment security, and young children's emotional knowledge in a high risk sample. *British Journal of Developmental Psychology, 24,* 89–104.

Raver, C. C. (2002). Emotions matter: Making the case for the role of young children's emotional development for early school readiness. *Social Policy Report, 16*(3), 13–19.

Raver, C. C. (2003). Does work pay psychologically as well as economically? The role of employment in predicting depressive symptoms and parenting among low-income families. *Child Development, 74*(6), 1720–1736.

Raver, C. C., Aber, J. L., & Gershoff, E. T. (2007). Testing equivalence of mediating models of income, parenting, and school readiness for White, Black, and Hispanic children in a national sample. *Child Development, 78*(1), 96–115.

Raver, C. C., Blackburn, E. K., Bancroft, M., & Torp, N. (1999). Relations between effective emotional self-regulation, attentional control, and low-income preschoolers' social competence with peers. *Early Education and Development, 10*(3), 334–350.

Raver, C. C., Garner, P. W., & Smith-Donald, R. (2007). The roles of emotion regulation and emotion knowledge for children's academic readiness: Are the links causal? In R. C. Pianta, M. J. Cox, & K. L. Snow (Eds.), *School readiness and the transition to kindergarten in the era of accountability* (pp. 121–148). Baltimore, MD: Paul H. Brookes.

Raver, C. C., Jones, S. M., Li-Grining, C. P., Metzger, M., Champion, K. M., & Sardin, L. (2008). Improving preschool classroom processes: Preliminary findings from a randomized trial implemented in Head Start settings. *Early Childhood Research Quarterly, 23*(1), 10–26. doi:10.1016/j.ecresq.2007.09.001

Raver, C. C., & Knitzer, J. (2002). *Ready to enter: What research tells policymakers about strategies to promote social and emotional school readiness among three- and four-year-old children.* New York: National Center for Children in Poverty. Retrieved from academiccommons.columbia.edu/catalog/ac:127551

Raver, C. C., Smith-Donald, R., Hayes, T., & Richardson, B. (2007). Preliminary construct and concurrent validity of the preschool self-regulation assessment (PSRA) for field-based research. *Early Childhood Research Quarterly, 22*, 173–187.

Raver, C. C., & Zigler, E. F. (1997). Social competence: An untapped dimension in evaluating Head Start's success. *Early Childhood Research Quarterly, 12*(4), 363–385.

Raver, C. C., & Zigler, E. F. (2004, January). Another step back?: Assessing readiness in Head Start. *Beyond the Journal: Young Children on the Web.* Retrieved from www.naeyc.org/files/yc/file/200401/Raver.pdf

Ray, A., Bowman, B., & Brownell, J.O. (2006). Teacher–child relationships, social–emotional development, and school achievement. In B. Bowman, Moore, E.K. (Ed.), *School readiness and social–emotional development: Perspectives on cultural diversity* (pp. 7–22). Washington, DC: National Black Child Development Institute.

Riggs, N. R., Greenberg, M. T., Kusché, C. A., & Pentz, M. A. (2006). The mediational role of neurocognition in the behavioral outcomes of a social–emotional prevention program in elementary school students: Effects of the PATHS curriculum. *Prevention Science, 7*(1), 91–102.

Riggs, N. R., Jahromi, L. B., Razza, R. P., Dillworth-Bart, J. E., & Mueller, U. (2006). Executive function and the promotion of social–emotional competence. *Journal of Applied Developmental Psychology, 27*, 300–306.

Ritchie, S., Maxwell, K., & Clifford, R. (2007). FirstSchool: A new vision for education. In R. C. Pianta, M. J. Cox, & K. L. Snow (Eds.), *School readiness and the transition to kindergarten in the era of accountability* (pp. 85–98). Baltimore, MD: Paul H. Brookes.

Rodriguez, J. L., Diaz, R. M., Duran, D., & Espinosa, L. (1995). The impact of bilingual preschool education on the language development of Spanish-speaking children. *Early Childhood Research Quarterly, 10*, 475–490.

Rothbart, M. K. (2011). *Becoming who we are: Temperament and personality in development.* New York, NY: Guilford Press.

Saarni, C. (1999). *The development of emotional competence.* New York, NY: Guilford Press.

Santos, R. M., & Ostrosky, M. M. (2007). *Understanding the impact of language differences on classroom behavior.* Retrieved from journal.naeyc.org/btj/200307/Understanding.pdf

Schultz, D., Izard, C. E., Ackerman, B. P., & Youngstrom, E. A. (2001). Emotion knowledge in economically disadvantaged children: Self-regulatory antecedents and relations to social difficulties and withdrawal. *Development and Psychopathology, 13*, 53–67.

Schunk, D. H., & Zimmerman, B. J. (1994). *Self-regulation of learning and performance: Issues and educational applications.* Hillsdale, NJ: Lawrence Erlbaum Associates.

Shonkoff, J. P., & Phillips, D. A. (Eds.). (2000). *From neurons to neighborhoods: The science of early childhood development.* Washington, DC: The National Academies Press.

Shulman, J., & Mesa-Bains, A. (1993). *Diversity in the classroom: A casebook for teachers and teacher educators.* Hillsdale, NJ: Research for Better Schools and Lawrence Erlbaum Associates.

Shulman, J. H., Lotan, R. A., & Whitcomb, J. A. (Eds.). (1998). *Facilitator's guide to groupwork in diverse classrooms: A casebook for educators.* New York, NY: Teachers College Press.

Shulman, J. H., & Sato, M. (Eds.). (2006). *Mentoring teachers toward excellence: Supporting and developing highly qualified teachers.* San Francisco, CA: Jossey-Bass and WestEd.

Shure, M. B., & Spivack, G. (1982). Interpersonal problem-solving in young children: A cognitive approach to prevention. *American Journal of Community Psychology, 10*(3), 341–356.

Singer, J. (2007). The Brazelton Touchpoints approach to infants and toddlers in care: Foundation for a lifetime of learning and loving. *Dimensions of Early Childhood, 35*(3), 4–11.

Skibbe, L. E., Connor, C. M., Morrison, F. J., & Jewkes, A. M. (2011). Schooling effects on preschoolers' self-regulation, early literacy, and language growth. *Early Childhood Research Quarterly, 26*(1), 42–49.

Smith-Donald, R., Raver, C. C., Hayes, T., & Richardson, B. (2007). Preliminary construct and concurrent validity of the Preschool Self-Regulation Assessment (PSRA) for field-based research. *Early Childhood Research Quarterly, 22*, 173–187.

Sparrow, J. D. (2007). Understanding stress in children. *Pediatric Annals, 36*(4), 187–193.

Sparrow, J. D. (2008). New approaches to optimizing child development and breaking the cycle of poverty. Retrieved from www.brazeltontouchpoints.org/wp-content/uploads/2011/09/Touchpoints_Theory_of_Change_Dec_2008.pdf

Stipek, D. J. (2002). *Motivation to learn: Integrating theory and practice* (4th ed.). Boston: Allyn & Bacon.

Stipek, D. J., & Seal, K. (2001). *Motivated minds: Raising children to love learning.* New York, NY: Henry Holt.

Stritikus, T. T., & García, E. E. (2005). Revisiting the bilingual debate from the perspectives of parents: Policy, practice, and matches or mismatches. *Educational Policy, 19*(5), 729–744.

Suárez-Orozco, C., & Suárez-Orozco, M. M. (2001). *Children of immigration.* Cambridge, MA: Harvard University Press.

Sudzina, M. R. (Ed.) (1999). *Case study applications for teacher education: Cases of teaching and learning in the content areas.* Boston, MA: Allyn & Bacon.

Sutton, R. E., & Wheatley, K. F. (2003). Teachers' emotions and teaching: A review of the literature and directions for future research. *Educational Psychology Review, 15*(4), 327–358.

Tamis-LeMonda, C. S., Way, N., Hughes, D., Yoshikawa, H., Kalman, R. K., & Niwa, E. Y. (2007). Parents' goals for children: The dynamic coexistence of individualism and collectivism in cultures and individuals. *Social Development, 17*(1), 183–209.

Tartell, E., Klein, S. M., & Jewett, J. L. (Eds.). (1998). *When teachers reflect: Journeys toward effective, inclusive practice.* Washington, DC: National Association for the Education of Young Children.

Thompson, R. A. (2002). The roots of school readiness in social and emotional development. In *Set for success: Building a strong foundation for school readiness based on the social-emotional development of young children* (pp. 8–29). The Kauffman Early Education Exchange (Vol. 1, no. 1). Kansas City, MO: The Ewing Marion Kauffman Foundation..

Thompson, R. A. (2004, November). Shaping the brains of tomorrow: What developmental science teaches about the importance of investing early in children. *The American Prospect, 15*(11), A16–A18.

Thompson, R. A. (2007). Conversation and developing understanding: Introduction to the Special Issue. *Merrill-Palmer Quarterly, 52*(1), 1–16.

Thompson, R. A., & Lagattuta, K. (2006). Feeling and understanding: Early emotional development. In K. M. D. Phillips (Ed.), *Blackwell handbook of early childhood development* (pp. 317–337). Malden, MA: Blackwell.

Thompson, R. A., Meyer, S., & McGinley, M. (2005). Understanding values in relationship: The development of conscience. In M. Killen & J. Smetana (Eds.), *Handbook of moral development* (pp. 267–289). Mahwah, NJ: Lawrence Erlbaum Associates.

Tobin, J. J., Wu, D. Y. H., & Davidson, D. H. (1989). *Preschool in three cultures: Japan, China, and the United States.* New Haven, CT: Yale University Press.

Tough, P. (2008). *Whatever it takes: Geoffrey Canada's quest to change Harlem and America.* New York, NY: Houghton Mifflin.

Tudge, J. R. H., Douct, F., Odero, D., Sperd, T. M., Piccinini, C. A., & Lopez, R. (2006). A window into different cultural worlds: Young children's everyday activities in the United States, Brazil, and Kenya. *Child Development, 77*(5), 1446–1469.

Tudge, J. R. H., Odero, D. A., Hogan, D. M., & Etz, K. E. (2003). Relations between the everyday activities of preschoolers and their teachers' perceptions of their competence in the first years of school. *Early Childhood Research Quarterly,*

18(1), 42–64.

Tye, B. B., & O'Brien, L. (2002). Why are experienced teachers leaving the profession? *Phi Delta Kappan, 84*(1), 24–32.

US. Department of Health and Human Services, Administration for Children and Families. (2017). *Head Start Program performance standards.* Retrieved from eclkc.ohs.acf.hhs.gov/policy/45-cfr-chap-xiii

Vandell, D. L., Nenide, L., & VanWinkle, S. G. (2006). Peer relationships in early childhood. In K. M. D. Phillips (Ed.), *Blackwell handbook of early childhood development* (pp. 455–470). Malden, MA: Blackwell.

Webster-Stratton, C. (1998). Preventing conduct problems in Head Start children: Strengthening parenting competencies. *Journal of Consulting and Clinical Psychology, 66*(5), 715–730.

Webster-Stratton, C., & Hammond, M. (1998). Conduct problems and level of social competence in Head Start children: Prevalence, pervasiveness, and associated risk factors. *Clinical Child and Family Review, 1*(2), 101–124.

Webster-Stratton, C., & Reid, M. J. (2004). Strengthening social and emotional competence in young children: The foundation for early school readiness and success. *Infants and Young Children, 17*(2), 96–113.

WestEd's Center for Child and Family Studies & California Department of Education, Child Development Division. (2007). *Preschool English learners: Principles and practices to promote language, literacy, and learning: A resource guide.* Sacramento, CA: California Department of Education.

WestEd's Center for Child and Family Studies & California Department of Education, Child Development Division. (2009). *Preschool English learners: Principles and practices to promote language, literacy, and learning: A resource guide* (2nd ed.). Sacramento, CA: California Department of Education.

Winsler, A., Diaz, R. M., Espinosa, L., & Rodriguez, J. L. (1999). When learning a second language does not mean losing the first: Bilingual language development in low-income, Spanish-speaking children attending bilingual preschool. *Child Development, 70*(2), 349–362.

Youngstrom, E., Wolpaw, J. M., Kogos, J. L., Schoff, K., Ackerman, B., & Izard, C. (2000). Interpersonal problem solving in preschool and first grade: Developmental change and ecological validity. *Journal of Clinical Child Psychology, 29*(4), 589–602.

Zhou, Q., Eisenberg, N., Wang, Y., & Reiser, M. (2004). Chinese children's effortful control and dispositional anger/frustration: Relations to parenting styles and children's social functioning. *Developmental Psychology, 40*, 352–366.

Zhou, Q., Lengua, L. J., & Wang, Y. (2009). The relations of temperament reactivity and regulation to children's adjustment problems in China and the United States. *Developmental Psychology, 45*, 764–781.

Zhou, Q., Main, A., & Wang, Y. (2010). The relations of temperamental effortful control and anger/frustration to Chinese children's academic achievement and social adjustment: A longitudinal study. *Journal of Educational Psychology, 102*(1), 180–196.

Zhou, Q., Sandler, I. N., Millsap, R. E., Wolchik, S. A., & Dawson-McClure, S. R. (2008). Mother–child relationship quality and effective discipline as mediators of the six-year effects of the New Beginnings Program for children from divorced families. *Journal of Consulting and Clinical Psychology, 76*, 579–594.

Zhou, Q., Wang, Y., Eisenberg, N., Wolchik, S., Tein, J.-Y., & Deng, X. (2008). Relations of parenting and temperament to Chinese children's experience of negative life events, coping efficacy, and externalizing problems. *Child Development, 79*, 493–513.

Zigler, E. (1979). Project Head Start: Success or failure? In E. Zigler & J. Valentine (Eds.), *Project Head Start: A legacy of the War on Poverty*. New York, NY: Free Press.

Zigler, E., & Bishop-Josef, S. J. (2004). Play under siege. In E. Zigler, D. G. Singer, & S. J. Bishop-Josef (Eds.), *Children's play: The roots of reading* (pp. 1–13). Washington DC: Zero to Three Press.

Zigler, E., Gilliam, W. S., & Jones, S. M. (2006). *A vision for universal preschool education*. New York, NY: Cambridge University Press.

Zigler, E., Gordic, B., & Styfco, S. J. (2007). What is the goal of Head Start? Four decades of confusion and debate. *NHSA Dialog: The Research-to-Practice Journal for the Early Childhood Field, 10*(2), 83–97.

Zigler, E., & Valentine, J. (1979). *Project Head Start: A legacy of the War on Poverty*. New York, NY: Free Press.

Zins, J. E., Bloodworth, M. R., Weissberg, R. P., & Walberg, H. J. (Eds.). (2004). *The scientific base linking social and emotional learning to school success*. New York, NY: Teachers College Press.

References

American Academy of Pediatrics, American Public Health Association, & National Resource Center for Health and Safety in Child Care and Early Education. (2011). *Caring for our children: National health and safety performance standards; Guidelines for early care and education programs* (3rd ed.). Elk Grove Village, IL: American Academy of Pediatrics; Washington, DC: American Public Health Association. Retrieved from cfoc.nrckids.org/

American Enterprise Institute for Public Policy Research and the Brookings Institution. (2015). *Opportunity, responsibility, and security: A consensus plan for reducing poverty and restoring the American dream.* Retrieved from www.brookings.edu/wp-content/uploads/2016/07/Full-Report.pdf

Angeli, C. (2004). The effects of case-based learning on early childhood pre-service teachers' beliefs about the pedagogical uses of ICT. *Journal of Educational Media, 29*(3), 139–151.

Barbarin, O. A., & Crawford, G. M. (2006). Acknowledging and reducing stigmatization of African American boys. *Young Children, 61*(6), 79–86.

Barbarin, O. A., Murry, V. M., Tolan, P., & Graham, S. (2016). Development of boys and young men of color: Implications of developmental science for My Brother's Keeper Initiative. *Social Policy Report, 29*(3), 1–31.

Barnett, C., & Tyson, P. A. (1999). Case methods and teacher change: Shifting authority to build autonomy. In M. A. Lundeberg, B. B. Levin, & H. L. Harrington (Eds.), *Who learns what from cases and how?: The research base for teaching and learning with cases* (pp. 53–70). Mahwah, NJ: Lawrence Erlbaum Associates.

Bodrova, E., & Leong, D. (2007). *Tools of the mind: The Vygotskian approach to early childhood education* (2nd ed.). Upper Saddle River, NJ: Pearson/Merrill Prentice Hall.

Brazelton, T. B., & Sparrow, J. D. (2001). *Touchpoints three to six: your child's emotional and behavioral development.* Cambridge, MA: Perseus.

Brazelton, T. B., & Sparrow, J. D. (2006). *Touchpoints—birth to three: Your child's emotional and behavioral development* (2nd ed.). Cambridge, MA: Da Capo Press.

Bruno, H. E. (2008). *Leading on purpose.* New York, NY: McGraw-Hill.

Bruno, H. E. (2012). *What you need to lead an early childhood program: Emotional intelligence in practice.* Washington, DC: National Association for the Education of Young Children.

California Department of Education. (2009). *Preschool English learners: Principles and practices to promote language, literacy, and learning—a resource guide* (2nd ed.). Sacramento, CA: California Department of Education.

Center for Disease Control and Prevention. (2016, April 1). Adverse childhood experiences(ACEs). Retrieved from www.cdc.gov/violenceprevention/acestudy/

Center for Early Education and Development. (2017). Classroom Assessment Scoring System (CLASS™). Retrieved from http://ceed.umn.edu/class/

Center for the Study of Child Care Employment. (n.d.). About us. Retrieved from cscce.berkeley.edu/about/

Center on the Developing Child at Harvard University. (2015). Executive function & self-regulation. Retrieved from developingchild.harvard.edu/science/key-concepts/executive-function/

Chess, S., & Thomas, A. (1996). *Temperament: Theory and practice.* New York, NY: Brunner / Mazel.

Chu, A. T., & Lieberman, A. F. (2010). Clinical implications of traumatic stress from birth to age five. *Annual Review of Clinical Psychology, 6,* 469–494. doi:10.1146/annurev.clinpsy.121208.131204

Cole, S. F., Greenwald O'Brien, J., Geron Gadd, M., Ristuccia, J., Wallace, D., & Gregory, M. (2005). *Helping traumatized children learn: Supportive school environments for children traumatized by family violence.* Boston, MA: Massachusetts Advocates for Children. Retrieved from www.k12.wa.us/CompassionateSchools/pubdocs/HelpTraumatizedChildLearn.pdf

Collaborative for Academic, Social, and Emotional Learning (CASEL). (2017a). About: History. Retrieved from www.casel.org/history /

Collaborative for Academic, Social, and Emotional Learning (CASEL). (2017b). About: Our work. Retrieved from www.casel.org/our-work/

Collaborative for Academic, Social, and Emotional Learning (CASEL). (2017c). Core SEL competencies. Retrieved from www.casel.org/core-competencies /

Collaborative for Academic, Social, and Emotional Learning (CASEL). (2017d). SEL impact. Retrieved from www.casel.org/impact/

Collaborative for Academic, Social, and Emotional Learning (CASEL). (2017e). What is SEL? Retrieved from www.casel.org/what-is-sel/

Collins, J. C. (2005). *Good to great and the social sectors: Why business thinking is not the answer: A monograph to accompany "Good to great."* New York, NY: Harper Collins.

Copple, C., & Bredekamp, S. (2009). *Developmentally appropriate practice in early childhood programs serving children from birth through age 8* (3rd ed.). Washington, DC: National Association for the Education of Young Children.

Craig, S. E . (2016). *Trauma-sensitive schools: Learning communities transforming children's lives, K–5.* New York, NY: Teachers College Press.

Daniels, S., & Piechowski, M. M. (2009). *Living with intensity: Emotional development of gifted children, adolescents, and adults.* Scottsdale, AZ: Great Potential Press.

Denham, S. A. (2006). Social–emotional competence as support for school readiness: What is it and how do we assess it? *Early Education and Development, 17*(1), 57–89.

Denham, S. A., & Burton, R. (2003). *Social and emotional prevention and intervention programming for preschoolers.* New York, NY: Kluwer Academic/Plenum.

Denham, S. A., & Weissberg, R. P. (2003). Social-emotional learning in early childhood: what we know and where to go from here. In E. Cheesebrough, P. King, T. P. Gullotta, & M. Bloom (Eds.), *A blueprint for the promotion of prosocial behavior in early childhood* (pp. 13-50). New York: Kluwer Academic/Plenum Publishers.

Derrick-Mills , T., Sandstrom, H., Pettijohn, S., Fyffe, S., & Koulish, J. (2014). *Data use for continuous quality improvement: What the Head Start field can learn from other disciplines: A literature review and conceptual framework* (OPRE Report # 2014-77). Washington, DC: Office of Planning, Research and Evaluation, Administration for Children and Families. U.S. Department of Health and Human Services.

Diamond, A., Barnett, W. S., Thomas, J., & Munro, S. (2007). Preschool program improves cognitive control. *Science, 318*(5855), 1387–1388. doi:10.1126/science.1151148

Frank Porter Graham Child Development Institute. (2017). *Environment Rating Scales: Early Childhood Environment Rating Scale (ECERS-R)*. Retrieved from ers.fpg.unc.edu/early-childhood-environment-rating-scale-ecers-r

Freedman, J. (2012). The six seconds EQ model. Retrieved from www.6seconds.org/2010/01/27/the-six-seconds-eq-model/

Gilliam, W. S. (2005). *Prekindergarteners Left Behind: Expulsion rates in state prekindergarten programs.* FCD Policy Brief Series, no. 3. New York, NY: Foundation for Child Development.

Gilliam, W . S., Maupin, A. N., Reyes, C. R., Accavitti, M., & Shic, F. (2016). *Do early educators' implicit bias regarding sex and race relate to behavior expectations and recommendations of preschool expulsions and suspensions?* New Haven, CT: Yale University Child Study Center. Retrieved from ziglercenter.yale.edu/publications/Preschool Implicit Bias Policy Brief_final_9_26_276766_5379.pdf

Gilliam, W. S., & Shahar , G. (2006). Preschool and child care expulsion and suspension: Rates and predictors in one state. *Infants & Young Children, 19*(3), 228–245. doi:10.1097/00001163-200607000-00007

Goffin, S. G. (2015). *Professionalizing early childhood education as a field of practice: A guide to the next era.* St. Paul, MN: Redleaf Press.

Goleman, D. (1995). *Emotional intelligence: Why it can matter more than IQ.* New York, NY: Bantam Books.

Goleman, D. (1998). *Working with emotional intelligence.* New York, NY: Bantam Books.

Goleman, D. (2003). *Destructive emotions: How can we overcome them?: A scientific collaboration with the Dalai Lama.* New York, NY: Bantam Books.

Goleman, D. (2004). What makes a leader? *Harvard Business Review, 82*(1), 82–91.

Goleman, D. (2013). *Focus : the hidden driver of excellence.* New York: Harper.

Goleman, D., Boyatzis, R. E., & McKee, A. (2002). *Primal leadership: Realizing the power of emotional intelligence.* Boston, MA.: Harvard Business School Press.

Gomez, R. E., Kagan, S. L., & Fox, E. A. (2015). Professional development of the early childhood education teaching workforce in the United States: An overview. *Professional Development in Education, 41*(2), 169–186. doi:10.1080/19415257.2014.986820

Gravett, S., de Beer, J., Odendaal-Kroon, R., & Merseth, K. K. (2017). The affordances of case-based teaching for the professional learning of student-teachers. *Journal of Curriculum Studies, 49*(3), 369–390. doi:10.1080/00220272.2016.1149224

Head Start Early Childhood Learning and Knowledge Center . (2016a). Designation renewal system. Retrieved from eclkc.ohs.acf.hhs.gov/hslc/grants/dr

Head Start Early Childhood Learning and Knowledge Center. (2016b). Directors & managers. Retrieved from eclkc.ohs.acf.hhs.gov/hslc/hs/sr/roles/dir-mgr

Head Start Early Childhood Learning and Knowledge Center. (2016c). Education managers. Retrieved from eclkc.ohs.acf.hhs.gov/hslc/hs/sr/roles/dir-mgr/ed-mgr.html

Head Start Early Childhood Learning and Knowledge Center. (2016d). Keep children safe using active supervision. Retrieved from eclkc.ohs.acf.hhs.gov/hslc/tta-system/health/safety-injury-prevention/safe-healthy-environments/active-supervision.html

Holmes, C., Levy, M., Smith, A., Pinne, S., & Neese, P. (2015). A model for creating a supportive trauma-informed culture for children in preschool settings. *Journal of Child and Family Studies, 24*(6), 1650–1659. doi:10.1007/s10826-014-9968-6

Hyson, M. (2004). *The emotional development of young children: Building an emotion-centered curriculum* (2nd ed.). New York, NY: Teachers College Press.

Hyson, M. (2008). *Enthusiastic and engaged learners: Approaches to learning in the early childhood classroom.* New York, NY & Washington, DC: Teachers College Press and National Association for the Education of Young Children.

Institute of Medicine & National Research Council. (2015). *Transforming the workforce for children birth through age 8: A unifying foundation.* Washington, DC: The National Academies Press.

Kagan, J., & Snidman, N. (2004). *The long shadow of temperament.* Cambridge, MA: Belknap Press of Harvard University Press.

Kaiser, B., & Rasminsky, J. S. (2017). *Challenging behavior in young children: Understanding, preventing, and responding effectively* (4th ed.). Boston, MA: Pearson.

Kinniburgh, K. J., Blaustein, M., & Spinazzola, J. (2005). Attachment, self-regulation, and competency: A comprehensive intervention framework for children with complex trauma. *Psychiatric Annals, 35*(5), 424–430.

Lee, K., & Choi, I. (2008). Learning classroom management through web-based case instruction: Implications for early childhood teacher education. *Early Childhood Education Journal, 35*(6), 495–503. doi:10.1007/s10643-008-0250-7

Levin, B. B. (1995). Using the case method in teacher education: The role of discussion and experience in teachers' thinking about cases. *Teaching and Teacher Education, 11*(1), 93–79.

Levin, B. B. (1999). The role of discussion in case pedagogy: Who learns what? And how. In M. A. Lundeberg, B. B. Levin, & H. L. Harrington (Eds.), *Who learns what from cases and how?: The research base for teaching and learning with cases* (pp. 139-157). Mahwah, NJ: Lawrence Erlbaum Associates.

Lieberman, A. F. (1993). *The emotional life of the toddler.* New York, NY: The Free Press.

Linder, S. M., Rembert, K., Simpson, A., & Ramey, M. D. (2016). A mixed-methods investigation of early childhood professional development for providers and recipients in the United States. *Professional Development in Education, 42*(1), 123–149. doi:10.1080/19415257.2014.978483

Lundeberg, M. A. (1999). Discovering teaching and learning through cases. In M. A.

Lundeberg, B. B. Levin, & H. L. Harrington (Eds.), *Who learns what from cases and how?: The research base for teaching and learning with cases* (pp. 3–24). Mahwah, NJ: Lawrence Erlbaum Associates.

Lynn, L. E. (1999). *Teaching and learning with cases: A guidebook.* New York, NY: Chatham House.

Mayer, J. D., Salovey, P., & Caruso, D. R. (2004). Emotional intelligence: Theory, findings, and implications. *Psychological Inquiry, 15*(3), 197–215. doi:10.1207/s15327965pli1503_02

Mead, S., & Mitchel, A. L. (2016). *Moneyball for Head Start: Using data, evidence, and evaluation to improve outcomes for children and families.* Washington, D]: Results for America, Bellwether Education Partners, National Head Start Association, and Volcker Alliance. Retrieved from www.nhsa.org/files/resources/moneyball_for_head_start_final.pdf

Merseth, K. K. (1996). Cases and the case method in teacher education. In J. P. Sikula, T. J. Buttery, E. Guyton, & Association of Teacher Educators (Eds.), *Handbook of research on teacher education* (2nd ed., pp. 722–746). New York, NY: Macmillan Library Reference.

Merseth, K. K. (1999). Foreword: A rationale for case-based pedagogy in teacher education. In M. A. Lundeberg, B. B. Levin, & H. L. Harrington (Eds.), *Who learns what from cases and how?: The research base for teaching and learning with cases* (pp. ix–xvi). Mahwah, NJ: Lawrence Erlbaum Associates.

Mongeau, L. (2013). Head Start requirement boosts college degrees for early childhood educators. Retrieved from edsource.org/2013/head-start-requirement-boosts-college-degrees-for-early-childhood-educators/25375

Nathanson, L., Rivers, S. E., Flynn, L. M., & Brackett, M. A. (2016). Creating emotionally intelligent schools with RULER. *Emotion Review, 8*(4), 305–310. doi:10.1177/1754073916650495

National Academy of Sciences. (2008). *Early childhood assessment: Why, what, and how.* Washington, DC: The National Academies Press.

National Association for the Education of Young Children (NAEYC). (2009). Where we stand on assessing young English language learners. Washington, DC: NAEYC. Retrieved from www.naeyc.org/files/naeyc/file/positions/WWSEnglishLanguageLearnersWeb.pdf

National Association for the Education of Young Children (NAEYC). (Feb. 24, 2012a). Engaging diverse families. Retrieved from www.naeyc.org/ecp/trainings/edf

National Association for the Education of Young Children (NAEYC). (2012b). *2010 NAEYC standards for initial & advanced early childhood professional preparation programs.* Washington, DC: NAEYC. Retrieved from www.naeyc.org/caep/files/caep/NAEYC Initial and Advanced Standards 10_2012.pdf

National Association for the Education of Young Children (NAEYC). (n.d.). Overview: power to the profession. Retrieved from www.naeyc.org/profession/overview

National Center on Early Childhood Quality Assurance. (n.d.). About QRIS. Retrieved from https://qrisguide.acf.hhs.gov/index.cfm?do=qrisabout

National Child Traumatic Stress Network (NCTSN). (2008). *Psychological and behavioral impact of trauma: Preschool children.* Retrieved from www.nctsn.org/products/psychological-and-behavioral-impact-trauma-preschool-children-2008

Nemeth, K. N., & Simon, F. S. (2013). Using technology as a teaching tool for dual language learners in preschool through grade 3. *Young Children, 68*(1), 48–52.

Nicholson, M. J., & Kroll, L. (2014). Developing leadership for early childhood professionals through oral inquiry: Strengthening equity through making particulars visible in dilemmas of practice. *Early Child Development and Care, 185,* 17–43.

PATHS® Training. (2011). The PATHS® Curriculum. Retrieved from www.pathstraining.com/main/curriculum/

Perry, B. D. (2006). Resilience: Where does it come from? In *Children and grief: Guidance and support resources.* Retrieved from www.scholastic.com/browse/article.jsp?id=3746847

Rand, M. K., & National Association for the Education of Young Children (NAEYC). (2000). *Giving it some thought: Cases for early childhood practice.* Washington, DC: NAEYC.

Salovey, P., & Mayer, J. D. (1990). Emotional intelligence. *Imagination, Cognition, and Personality, 9*(3), 185–211.

Schiano, W., & Anderson, E. (2014). *Teaching with cases: A practical guide.* Boston, MA: Harvard Business School.

Shulman, J. H. (1992). *Tender feelings, hidden thoughts: Confronting bias, innocence, and racism through case discussions* [Revised]. Paper presented at the annual meeting of the American Educational Research Association (AERA), San Francisco, CA.

Shulman, J. H., Whittaker, A., & Lew, M. (2002). *Using assessments to teach for understanding: A casebook for educators.* New York, NY: Teachers College Press.

Snyder, P., & McWilliam, P. J. (2003). Using case method of instruction effectively in early intervention personnel preparation. *Infants and Young Children, 16*(4), 284–295.

Tools of the Mind. (2017). What is Tools? Retrieved from toolsofthemind.org/learn/what-is-tools/

Tsai, J. L. (2007). Ideal affect: Cultural causes and behavioral consequences. *Perspectives on Psychological Science, 2*(3), 242–259. doi:10.1111/j.1745-6916.2007.00043.x

Tsai, J. L., Louie , J. Y., Chen, E. E., & Uchida, Y. (2007). Learning what feelings to desire: Socialization of ideal affect through children's storybooks. *Personality and Social Psychology Bulletin, 33*(1), 17–30.

Tsai, J. L., Miao, F. F., Seppala, E., Fung, H. H., & Yeung, D. Y. (2007). Influence and adjustment goals: Sources of cultural differences in ideal affect. *Journal of Personality and Social Psychology, 92*(6), 1102–1117.

U.S. Department of Health and Human Services, Administration for Children and Families. (2014). Trends in childcare center licensing regulations and policies for 2014. Retrieved from childcareta.acf.hhs.gov/resource/research-brief-1-trends-child-care-center-licensing-regulations-and-policies-2014

U.S. Department of Health and Human Services Administration for Children and Families. (2016). Head Start Policy & Regulations. Head Start Early Childhood Learning and Knowledge Center. Retrieved from eclkc.ohs.acf.hhs.gov/policy/45-cfr-chap-xiii

U.S. Department of Health and Human Services, Administration for Children and Families. (2017). Head Start Program performance standards. Retrieved from eclkc.ohs.acf.hhs.gov/policy/45-cfr-chap-xiii

Vygotsky, L. (1978). The role of play in development. In *Mind in Society: The development of higher psychological processes* (M. Cole, Trans., pp. 92–104). Cambridge MA: Harvard University Press.

Washington, V., Gadson, B., & Amel, K. L. (2015). *The new early childhood professional: A step-by-step guide to overcoming Goliath*. New York, NY: Teachers College Press.

Wassermann, S. (1994). *Introduction to case method teaching: A guide to the galaxy*. New York, NY: Teachers College Press.

Whitebook, M., Phillips, D., & Howes, C. (2014). Worthy work, STILL unlivable wages: The early childhood workforce 25 years after the National Child Care Staffing Study. Berkeley, CA: Center for the Study of Child Care Employment, University of California, Berkeley. Retrieved from cscce.berkeley.edu/files/2014/ReportFINAL.pdf

Yoshikawa, H., Weiland, C., Brooks-Gunn, J., Burchinal, M., Espinosa, L., Gormley, W. T., . . . Zaslow, M. (2013). *Investing in our future: The evidence base on preschool*. Washington, DC: Society for Research in Child Development.

Index

Abenavoli, R. M., 74
Abuse and trauma. *See* Trauma and
    abuse
Accavitti, M., 57–58, 60
Accountability movement, 7
Achievement gap, 7
Active students. *See* Case 3: "Sky-High
    Energy in Classroom Five"
ADHD, 59. *See also* Case 3: "Sky-High
    Energy in Classroom Five"
Administration for Children and
    Families, U.S. Department of
    Health and Human Services, xii,
    16, 59, 60, 77–78, 80, 96
Adverse Childhood Experience (ACE)
    study (Center for Disease Control
    and Prevention), 15, 72, 73
African American boys. *See* Case 3:
    "Sky-High Energy in Classroom
    Five"
Aggression. *See* Case 3: "Sky-High
    Energy in Classroom Five"
Alcoholism. *See* Case 4: "Roberto and
    Maria: Two Children dealing with
    Trauma"
Alexis, Sahara, 79–80. *See also* Case
    5: "Coming To Ground"; Case 6:
    "Crises and Compassion"
All Our Children Head Start Agency
    Cesar Chavez Center licensing (*See*
    Case 5: "Coming To Ground")
    described, 15–17, 78–79, 98–99
    leadership retreat (*See* Case 6:
    "Crises and Compassion")
Amel, K. L., 16, 95, 111–112, 114

American Academy of Pediatrics, 89n,
    96
American Enterprise Institute for Public
    Policy Research, 9
American Public Health Association,
    89n, 96
Anda, R. F., 73
Anderson, E., 4
Anderson, Shavaun. *See* Case 4:
    "Roberto and Maria: Two
    Children dealing with Trauma"
Angeli, C., 3
Antaramian, S., 61
Antigua, Martina. *See* Case 4: "Roberto
    and Maria: Two Children dealing
    with Trauma"
Appleton, J. J., 61
Art activities. *See* Case 3: "Sky-High
    Energy in Classroom Five"
Arvidson, J., 73
Asian Americans. *See also* Case 2:
    "Ming: A Mystery Story for
    Teachers and Student Teachers"
Asian Interest Forum, National
    Association for the Education of
    Young Children (NAEYC), 13, 37
Assessment and rating scales, 96
    CLASS (Classroom Assessment
    Scoring System), 81, 81n, 83, 83n,
    84, 91, 98
    Early Childhood Environment
    Rating Scale (ECERS), 84, 84n
    Quality Rating Improvement System
    (QRIS), 80, 81, 85, 90, 91, 98
Atkins-Burnett, S., 115

Case method of instruction
  best practices for, 2, 4–6
  case overviews, 11–17 (*See also*
    specific cases)
  classroom discussions, 5–6
  class size, 5
  developing new cases, 6
  development for early childhood
    education, 1–2
  in early childhood teacher education,
    3–4
  focus on emotional intelligence in,
    7–11
  instructor preparation for, 5–6
  nature of teaching cases, 2–3
  in professional development
    approach, 1–6
  study group discussions, 5
  using Recommended Readings, 3
  using Resources for Delving Deeper,
    3, 6
Center for Disease Control and
  Prevention, Adverse Childhood
  Experience (ACE) Study, 15, 72, 73
Center for Early Education and
  Development, 81n, 83n
Center for Emotional Intelligence, Yale
  University, 10, 67
Center for the Study of Child Care
  Employment, University of
  California at Berkeley, 14, 17, 104,
  104n, 115
Center on the Developing Child,
  Harvard University, 14, 56, 58
Center on the Social and Emotional
  Foundations for Early Learning,
  60
Cesar Chavez Center. *See also* Case 5:
  "Coming To Ground"
  described, 78–79
*Challenging Behavior in Young
  Children* (Kaiser & Rasminsky),
  14, 47, 57, 59
Chang, F., 27
Chazan-Cohen, R., 59
Chen, E. E., 13, 39, 40
Chess, Stella, 36, 39
Child abuse and trauma. *See* Case

4: "Roberto and Maria: Two
    Children dealing with Trauma"
Children First Inc. Preschool. *See also*
  Case 3: "Sky-High Energy in
  Classroom Five"
  described, 42
Children's Health Trust, 54–55, 58
Chinese Americans. *See also* Case
  2: "Ming: A Mystery Story for
  Teachers and Student Teachers"
  Asian Interest Forum, National
  Association for the Education of
  Young Children (NAEYC), 13, 37
Choi, I., 3
Chu, A. T., 15, 73
Cicchetti, D., 73
Clarke Brown, K., 114
CLASS (Classroom Assessment Scoring
  System), 81, 81n, 83, 83n, 84, 91,
  98
Clifford, R. M., 96
Coccia, M. A., 74
Cohen, G. L., 60
Cohen, J. A., 74
Cole, S. F., 15, 74
Collaborative for Academic, Social,
  and Emotional Learning (CASEL),
  8–10, 92–93, 96, 115
  CASEL framework for emotional
    and social intelligence, xvi, 10, 16,
    25
  founding of, 8–9
  role of, 9
Collins, James C., 16, 93, 95
Compensation of teachers, xix, 14, 15,
  16–17, 90, 97, 101, 103–104, 114
Competence Model (Peters), 21, 24–27
Conflict resolution. *See* Case 1:
  "Tomas, Arthur, and Sharing:
  Resolving Conflicts"
Content managers, xviii
Copple, C., 7, 27, 31, 37, 39, 49, 59
Craig, S. E., 15, 74
Crawford, G. M., 14, 27, 58
Cryer, D., 96
Cultural sensitivity. *See* Case 1:
  "Tomas, Arthur, and Sharing:
  Resolving Conflicts"; Case 2:

Yale University
  Center for Emotional Intelligence,
    10, 67
  Edward Zigler Center for Child
    Development and Social Policy, xii
Yeh, Chia-wa, xvii
Yeung, D. Y., 13
York Susanna. *See* Case 3: "Sky-High
  Energy in Classroom Five"
Yoshikawa, H., 4

Zaslow, M., 4
Zero to Six Collaborative Group, 73
Zero to Three, xii
Zigler, Edward, xi–xiii, xvi
Zinsser, K. M., 59–61
Zuckerman, Barry, 72

About the Author
and the Contributors

Peggy Daly Pizzo is the director of the Early Learning Project at the Stanford Graduate School of Education. Her decades of commitment to early care and education has taken her from teacher's assistant to White House policymaker and then researcher affiliated with Yale, Harvard, and Stanford Universities. She has worked at national organizations including Zero to Three; as a special assistant to the Commissioner of the Administration for Children, Youth, and Families; and as a member of the White House domestic policy staff. She has been an instructor in the department of psychiatry at Harvard Medical School and an affiliate faculty at what is now known as the Zigler Center for Child Development and Social Policy at Yale University. She has authored two books, numerous textbook chapters, and articles about policy and practice related to early care and education. She holds master's degrees from Tufts University and from the Harvard Graduate School of Education.

Teresa Gonczy O'Rourke is an early childhood policy and research consultant for systems-level organizations in California and Oregon. She has over 12 years of experience in education as a teacher and administrator, with a masters in policy and management from the Harvard Graduate School of Education.

Ed Greene is currently vice president for Partnerships and Community Development for Hispanic Information and Telecommunications Network (HITN) in Brooklyn, New York. Over his 40-year career, Ed has worked directly with infants, toddlers, preschool children, adolescents and families, as well as in a variety of leadership roles and capacities in philanthropic, private, and public sectors, and in higher education. He is a former elected board member of the National Association for the Education of Young Children and the High/Scope Educational Research Foundation, and currently serves as a trustee of the Coalition for Quality Children's Media.